MORE TALES OF *THE* OLD
COUNTRYMEN

Brian P. Martin

MORE TALES OF
THE OLD
COUNTRYMEN

DAVID & CHARLES

BY THE SAME AUTHOR

Tales of the Old Countrymen
Tales of the Old Gamekeepers
More Tales of the Old Gamekeepers
Tales of Time and Tide: *Stories of Life on Britain's Coasts*
Birds of Prey of the British Isles
Wildfowl of the British Isles & North-West Europe
Sporting Birds of Britain and Ireland
The Glorious Grouse
World Birds (Guinness)
The Great Shoots: *Britain's Premier Sporting Estates*
British Gameshooting, Roughshooting and Wildfowling
Game Cook/The Art of Game Cookery (with Rosemary Wadey)
The Pheasant – Studies in Words and Pictures

Illustrations by Philip Murphy

A DAVID & CHARLES BOOK

First published in the UK in 1996

A catalogue record for this book is available from the British Library.

ISBN 0 7153 0159 4

Typeset by ABM Typographics Limited Hull
and printed in Great Britain
by Butler & Tanner Ltd
for David & Charles
Brunel House   Newton Abbot   Devon

CONTENTS

INTRODUCTION

As I write this on a golden October morning, goldfinches are teasing seeds from the teasel heads just a few feet from my window. They are enjoying the fruits of a maturing year, just as the elderly characters in this book now harvest the fruits and memories of mature lives. But these birds and men have much more in common. Species such as finches and teasels, which depend on ill-named 'marginal' or 'waste'-land, have only held on in the manicured landscape of the twentieth century because of the sympathetic way in which old countrymen such as these have worked *with* nature, rather than sought to subjugate it. It is only very recently, with the flowering of the conservation movement, that we have come fully to appreciate the value of their old ways.

But these stalwarts offer much more than lessons in sustainable natural resources and wildlife management. They also show us a better social side to country life, how the average village once blossomed with real friends rather than mere neighbours, and how contentment seemed much more widespread – ironically during times of far greater austerity and hardship. They expected relatively little and, through mastering self-sufficiency, consumed relatively little. They made their own amusement and kept smiling through war as well as peace.

The thirteen characters in my book *Tales of the Old Countrymen* came almost entirely from very humble backgrounds and employed predominantly practical skills. But to be a true countryman it is by no means essential always to be poor, to have dirt under your fingernails and a face like a walnut shell. Much more important is a deep love of the out-

(Opposite) Lewis Blencowe: a true countryman

7

doors, and a genuinely caring attitude towards the landscape and both the wildlife and people who share it. The seventeen men I have chosen for this second 'countrymen' book have demonstrated these qualities through the power of the pen and the spoken word as well as the ploughshare. For example, country solicitor Paul Ryan has upheld the land rights of neighbours as skilfully as farming parson William Tavernor once ministered to both human and animal flocks. Both are as much countrymen as those who have spent their entire working lives turning the sod, and whether they survive through degrees of education or degrees of instinct is unimportant.

Five of my characters are in their seventies, nine in their eighties and three in their nineties, yet most remain exceptionally active. Eighty-three-year-old Harry Edge still drives a cattle lorry for a living, while 90-year-old Ivan Birley continues to lay hedges for the benefit of wildlife as well as farming, and 97-year-old George Ebdon still digs his garden and pickles his produce. All have taken immense pride in their work.

As well as describing mostly very different occupations from those in my first 'countrymen' book, I have visited many different corners of the British Isles. Most significantly, for the first time one of the *Tales* series of books includes Ireland. Fourteen Irish counties feature alongside nineteen on the UK mainland.

Every time I go to Ireland I imagine how good it would be to live there permanently, with so much relatively unspoilt countryside per head of population. I have no doubt that this space and the freedom it gives have done much to generate the internationally renowned warmth and charm of the Irish people, for land is at the base of Irish life. I hope that this special character is fully reflected in the five chapters devoted to Irishmen, but also that all readers both sides of the Irish Sea will enjoy discovering common bondage as well as local flavour. Surely a countryman is a countryman whether he lives in Ireland, Ulster, England or anywhere else.

These men have seen more dramatic change than any other generation. Those who were once the bedrock of a great empire, who dug for victory through two world wars and instinctively appreciated the role of fallow fields, now struggle to comprehend the bureaucracy of wine lakes, butter mountains and set-aside land. Where they once bowled a hoop up the high street, their grandchildren now parade in smart cars, and their admirable art of letter-writing has been sacrificed to the many-faced god of instant communication. For most of them, manners and respect in others are things of the past. Today, mobile-phonees have no time to sit and contemplate more gentle times. No wonder, then, that in the heart of Shakespeare country Brian Forsyth says: 'I think I've seen the best of England'; and in distant, unspoilt Mayo Michael Connolly's eyes fill with tears when he considers all that his son is missing in London. But neither man, nor any other in this book, is giving up without a fight for all the virtues which have sustained them so well.

Of course there will always be change, and always men such as these whose ways and occupations are mostly things of the past, but their inspiration in adaptation and survival is something which today's young lions will do well to emulate. Yes, this book is based literally on the language of yesteryear, but I believe that it enshrines much of the hope for tomorrow.

BRIAN P. MARTIN
Brook, Surrey

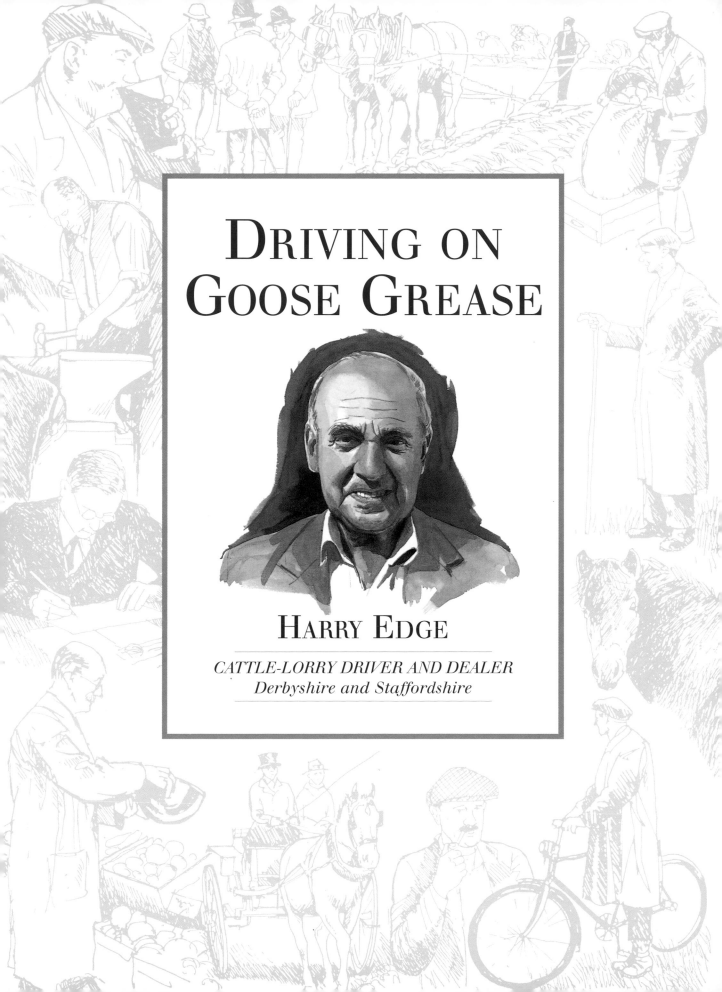

DRIVING ON GOOSE GREASE

HARRY EDGE

CATTLE-LORRY DRIVER AND DEALER
Derbyshire and Staffordshire

The Edge family at Fidler's Farm, where Harry was born

'Last month a chap comes into Uttoxeter market and says to me: "How much for a bullock, Harry?" I says: "Depends on the whether." "Weather?" he says. "Yes," I says: "whether or not I'm *buying* it off you or whether I'm *selling* it to you!".'

At an age when most people have given up driving even a light car for leisure, 83-year-old Harry Edge makes a living from taking cows and other farm animals to market aboard his lorry, just as he has done for over half a century. And despite bearing both the physical and emotional scars of a tough early life, he soldiers on with undiminished humour and business acumen. One of the most popular characters on the Derbyshire–Staffordshire border, he continues to take on cargoes of surprising variety. To him 'every day is a delight'. He has no plans to retire because 'as soon as you stop movin' they measure you up for that ol' box'.

One of five children, Henry Edge was born on 12 September 1912 at Fidler's Farm, West Broughton, Sudbury in Derbyshire, where his father rented some fifty acres from Lord Vernon. Harry's earliest memory is of 'working at home for nowt', as did most farmers' sons of the time. 'From the age of about eight I did the usual things, like milkin' cows by lantern-light before school, pulpin' mangolds for cattle feed, drivin' a horse and float and walkin' animals into Uttoxeter market. And no matter how tired you were, you still 'ad to walk the four miles into Sudbury village school.

'Father used to rear these Easter calves for veal, and another thing that always sticks in me mind is when we 'ad a lot of trouble gettin' these two great big calves onto the float for market. We 'ad this Irishman used to come round to 'elp, and when everyone was talkin' about the problem in the pub that evening he said: "Sure, we 'ad 'im in the corner and 'e wasn't there".'

While a schoolboy, and even after when working for his father, Harry only ever had a little 'pocket money' when muck-spreading for other people:

I got ha'penny a ruck (heap). The rucks were put out by horse and cart, and in those days the farmers took great pride in puttin' the rucks out in absolutely straight lines.

It cost 'alf a crown a year to join the Reading Room at Sudbury, and it was the hardest job in the world to get that money. You 'ad to be keen all right. There weren't no girls allowed in and I didn't go there to read, but I had great fun playin' rings, dominoes and billiards. When the greengrocer came down we used to raid 'is cart, which he left outside. And if 'e didn't come for a while we'd ride our bikes alongside his cart fillin' our pockets.

Another trick we played was on the landlord of the Vernon Arms. We used to give 'im a ten bob note for a tuppenny chocolate bar and when he gave us the change we'd say: 'Excuse me, Mr Jackson, but it was a pound I gave you.' Then he'd say: 'I'm sorry' and we'd go off with a big profit as well as the sweets. But all this was part of survival in those days.

We used to get clay from the side of the brook and make a pipe, using a hollow kedlock stem to suck through. We smoked the nub ends [cigarette butts] which we picked up off the road on the way to school. That cured me of smokin', and I've never taken it up since.

Birds'-nesting was a favourite pastime and I'd go right up to the crows' nests in the big firs. I'd put the eggs in me cap, and didn't care 'ow 'igh I went. And to reach the eggs of the water-hen [moorhen] we 'ad a stick with a spoon on the end. They made a good meal.

Despite his lifelong involvement with animals, Harry was not too keen on ferreting:

We did a lot of it as lads, but if a rabbit came out I used to kick it back down the 'ole till it went out me brother's side 'cos they always used to bite me. He was all right because he bred cony rabbits and knew how to handle them.

As lads we used to go out on a Friday to stop up fox holes for the Meynell Hunt, which went out Saturday. And when me and Wilson Jefferies were doin' this down Lake Bank we 'elped ourselves to a few of the rabbits before the fox got 'em. But the farmer's son, Ernie Deville, got wind of it and decided to give us a scare. One night 'e came down with a sheet over 'is 'ead, just like a ghost, and frightened poor Wilson 'alf to death. There must 'ave been some muck in 'is pants that night! We didn't get paid for helping the Hunt, but we all got a good feed at the earthstoppers' dinner.

We used to rabbit with a terrier cross collie, which was a great hunter. And old Deville 'ad these two blue merle dogs which could tear a fox to bits in no time, but they weren't too quick, so Jefferies' greyhound had to knock the fox over and slow it up a bit first.

Among Harry's favourite foods were his mother's home-made pork pies. 'She made wonderful scratchings too, not like the things you get now: they're 'ard as iron and no use to anyone. Each time a nearby farm killed a pig they'd always give you some of the meat. Everyone did this in turn because there weren't no freezers then and you didn't all kill your animals at the same time.

'We 'ad a wonderful 'orse to take us to market. Even with Mum and Dad up front and two calves on the back of the float 'e wouldn't walk an inch: 'e'd trot all the fourteen miles into Derby market. Lord Wordsworth used to chuck 'is cheque book down and say, name your price. He'd 'ave give us anythin' we'd want for that 'orse.'

As most old folk will testify, during the early twentieth century there was generally far greater discipline than there is nowadays. The Edge household was no exception:

It were a sin if me dad was up past five of a morning, and 'e didn't 'ave to shout twice for us kids at a quarter to six.

Every morning the first thing me Dad did was brew the tea. One day, as he was putting the kettle on 'e looked out and saw this chap striding across the field with a white stick. A few minutes later there was a knock on the door. It was 'im. He must have seen the smoke from the fire when Dad lit up and 'ad come for a brew. Obviously 'e wasn't as blind as 'e made out!

At school they'd give you the stick for ought. And it was no good tellin' your dad as he'd say: 'You must 'ave done somethin' to get it,' and then 'e'd give 'e another one.

It was just as bad outdoors because any nobs you saw in huntin' red coats and top hats used to 'it you on the 'ead with their riding crop if you didn't run to open the gate for 'em. And again, there was no point in tellin' your dad, as these men were our fathers' landlords and would soon 'ave 'em out if they caused trouble.

But no amount of discipline could stop young Edge having a lot of fun. Ever a practical joker, he once loosened all the corks in the vinegar bottles at the local fish and chips shop. As one lad shook a bottle, Harry engaged him in conversation until his chips were floating in vinegar.

'All our friends was about the same, poor; though as the eldest son in the house I was relatively well off, because for the others it was always hand-me-downs. Then one day me brother said about these trousers, "I'm not 'avin' those with six patches on one 'ole!" But boots were much better then, and could be repaired any amount of times. We got our hobnails from Griffin at Stramshall and even played football in 'em.

'At school, where all the kids called me Ben, we never thought of ought but farming, so when I left at fourteen I just worked for Father.'

When Harry was twenty he married Mildred, a local farmer's daughter. 'When we left to work for Mr Boley at Swarkestone Bridge, near Derby, all we 'ad was a few sticks from each house. But my first-ever wage of forty-five bob [£2 25p] a week was five bob [25p] better than most others, as I was a farmer's son. We had our first boy when I was just twenty-one, but lost him at twenty-four months.'

At Swarkestone one of Harry's jobs was to help four other men with milking the cows, a job which was not always straightforward:

Goin' down the cow shed I saw all these sharp hedge stakes lined up against the wall and wondered what they were for. Then one day this cow kicked Boley while 'e was milkin' and 'e picked up one of these sticks and whacked the cow with it three or four times till it kept its leg up in the air. 'It can't kick me now,' 'e said.

Some of the other men were very crafty, too. If they knewed there's a hard-milched cow – a kicker – in the line, they'd hold back while I finished so they wouldn't get it. But that made me cross because I didn't mind which cow I 'ad and all I wanted to do was finish the job.

One day I milked the front two quarters of this cow and everything was all right, but when I went to the back – wham! – the cow kicked me leg and the bucket and spilt the milk all over the place. So I picked up the milkin' stool and 'it the cow on the 'ead so 'ard the top of the stool flew off and landed in the hay bin. Just then Boley came in and 'ad a right go at me.

Next morning I left this cow for 'im to 'ave a go, and the same thing happened. He did the front two quarters OK, but when 'e moved to the back 'e was kicked so 'ard 'e went headlong in the muck. Afterwards that cow was always left for me to do, and when I left the farm that beast went to market the very next day!

There was a hundred acres of wheat on the farm and I had to carry eighteen-stone railway sacks of corn off the drum of the thrashing machine. They were weighed on scales, then I 'ad to wind them up on a hoist high enough to get 'em on me back and carry them up the steps into the corn loft. When the lorry came I 'ad to get them down again. One driver always used to say: 'Just one more, and then . . .'. 'And then what?' we'd say. 'And then another . . .' he'd reply. I tell you, after three weeks of that I 'ad shoulders like raw meat.

After two years at Swarkestone Harry had to take charge at his father-in-law's farm, at Waldley, near Doveridge:

My father-in-law went funny; 'e was up to 'is ears in debt. He used to get up at night and walk about the fields, so I 'ad to follow 'im round to make sure 'e was all right. There was this pit where milk used to be kept cool and he used to get a bucket and milking stool and walk round and round it for hours on end.

One morning when I fetched the cows up for milkin' I noticed that we 'ad a strange one among 'em. We left it there and went and 'ad breakfast. Afterwards me brother-in-law milked it and when we turned down the lane we met this lad and 'e said: ' 'ave you seen our cow?' 'Yes,' we said.

Later on when we gave the cow back they said: ' 'ave you milked it?' 'Yes,' we said, as it couldn't be left like that. But do you know what? Later on they said to our friend Jack Dyche: 'What do you think of Mr Edge? 'e milked our cow and we waited till eleven to see if he'd bring the milk down.' Talk about mean! And in any case, 'ow could we 'ave measured out that cow's exact quantity?

After eighteen months Harry had made great improvements and almost paid off all the debts. But sadly, his father-in-law was too unwell to sign the appropriate papers and the mortgage was foreclosed. So Harry left farming and took a job digging road footings.

Only nine months later, at the age of twenty-four, Harry was glad to become a farm worker for Arthur Trafford because there was a house with the job at Rocester, and that is where he still lives. Trafford was a cattle dealer and the stock came by lorry and train from markets all over the country. 'Trafford's son ran off with some of the market money, so his father threw him out and put his daughter on driving; but she couldn't manage, so he got me to go with the lorry. But then I got so behind with my other work Trafford called in Harry Heppinstall to plough my field. Harry 'ad the first up-and-down plough in the area, but 'e made such a mess of it, I 'ad to go and do it again with three horses to get it fine enough for sowing. It took me all day to level it with the harrow.'

Harry taught himself to drive, and for the first two years he had no licence at all. Then he had three provisional licences before being given a full licence, in the days when it was not necessary to take a test. Those early years were more carefree altogether, 'when you drove on string, and it didn't matter what condition the vehicle was in, as long as it went!' Not surprisingly, Harry had his fair share of excitement on the road:

We used to move animals with bombs droppin' all around us in the war, but I was more worried the time I was drivin' down Swinscoe Hill in the early forties. Trafford's Bedford had a dodgy gear lever which used to jump out – 'is daughter Betty could put it in again, but I couldn't, and I was scared stiff it would 'appen comin' down that steep hill as it was the first time on me own.

Partway down I thought I was goin' a bit 'ard so I put me foot on the brake and she steadied, and then I did the same again. But then she went right away and wouldn't stop. I was in top gear and the brake was red hot. Goin' full bore I couldn't turn on the curve where I wanted to and 'ad to go a mile along the flat before I could stop.

I was always in a rush. Trafford would tell six or seven farmers I'd be there at ha'past nine, so when I got there at ha'past eight they'd say: 'Why are you so early?' And when I got there at ha'past ten they'd say: 'Why are you so late?'

On other occasions it was the customers who made Harry late.

Once I took Mr Smith of Combridge to fetch his stallion from Lord Kenyon's. On the way home he said: 'We'll go and have a drink, Harry.' But I was drivin' and only 'ad 'alf of mild. In the meantime Smith was goin' around all the tables and makin' a real nuisance of 'imself, havin' a drink with everybody, and we were there quite a while. So when we got back Mrs Smith roared out and said to me: 'Will you have a drink, Edge, or have you had enough for one night?'

14

Harry outside the lodge in Rocester where he has lived since 1936

'I 'ad to put a rope around its neck to pull it out!'

In 1947 Trafford died suddenly at Ashbourne market. Harry took his coffin and flowers 'on a Ford flat-bed lorry to the funeral at Bradbourne. It was a hell of a journey – the snow was so deep that year some folks went about on skis.'

Harry then bought the lodge he lived in for £650, as well as a small field alongside and a Ford 4D flat-bed lorry which he put a cattle-box on. Local farmers were happy for him to continue with the business which he had already been doing for years, mainly taking their cattle to markets such as Chelford, Derby, Leek, Uttoxeter, Ashbourne, Newcastle-under-Lyme and Stone. He also started dealing in animals, which he does to this day. In his own words:

If there was a profit in it, I dealt in 'em. I've 'ad everythin' from cows to rabbits, horses to deer. Only the other day I 'ad a load of loose hens in the back. That woman ought to be locked up for keepin' 'em like that, filthy and with 'alf their feathers pecked out.

I often used to buy a pig at Derby on a Friday, but my old cattle lorry wouldn't go under the railway bridge out the back here. So I used to unload the pig and walk it up to the building. But one day when I was doin' this the pig shot off into the bushes and fell into the lake. I 'ad to put a rope round its neck to pull it out so it was squealin' its 'ead off, and I was supposed to be doin' this on the quiet as rationing was on.

We always did this at night, with Sid Harvey as lookout down here at the house. Everybody knew it went on. The local ministry men used to tell us when not to do 'em in return for a piece of pork. And even the superintendent of police from Stafford used to come up in a bloody great shooting brake for his cut, too.

But there was one time we 'ad a real scare. We killed a pig in the Anderson shelter out the back and brought it in here for Harry Ratcliffe the butcher to cut up. All of a sudden there was a knock on the door: it was the local bobby. There'd been an accident. A big fat woman had come off the back of a motorbike and had bones stickin' out her knee. The bobby wanted to know if they could bring her in while they waited for help. Well, we thought we're for it, now.

Luckily the accident was up the road a bit, and while they fetched the woman, my wife and

'All of a sudden there was a knock on the door . . .'

In 1949 Harry was going up Buxton Hill to Ashbourne market
when his lorry crankshaft broke

me gathered up all the bits of pig – and they were great big animals in those days – and took them through into the sitting-room, where we just threw them down on the carpet. We also 'ad to get all the blood and muck off the table.

Then they brought the woman in and put her on the sofa in the room between the kitchen and the sitting-room; and then I noticed a pig's leg, which we must have dropped in the rush, underneath the very seat where she lay. I thought, this is it, now we're done; but it turned out that you could only just see the trotter from a certain angle, and the bobby went off with the woman none the wiser. That was the biggest scare we ever had.

But there was one pig which came to us without any trouble. I found this lost piglet which someone must have dropped on the way to market and me missus reared it as a pet.

When it came to curing hams Harry was very particular. 'I rubbed the rind with a mixture of vinegar and brown sugar, followed by salt. Then I'd turn the meat face up, put salt all over it and rub saltpetre around the bone, which cures the bone part and stops it goin' wrong.'

Another illicit night-time activity which Harry often used to take part in was poaching hares: 'We mostly went lamping in a car with a shotgun and the roof back. It was my job to rush out and pick 'em up, and if you 'ad four on a stick it was as much as you could carry.'

Certain clothing was also greatly sought after during rationing. But Harry and his friends could always rely on the Irishman MacRice to bring silk cloth and stockings, hidden among the bales of straw when he came over with cattle for market. Sweets were easier to come by: 'We often had gypsies come round and sell me their toffee rations for the kids. One of them fancied a horse I had in the field by the road. "How about a straight chop?" 'e said. So 'e took me down to see 'is pony. "What do you 'ave in mind?" I asked. "A straight chop," he said again. But he didn't want to give me any meat. What he was suggesting was a *swap*. But I didn't agree.'

In 1949 Harry was going up Buxton Hill to Ashbourne market when his lorry crank-shaft broke:

I jammed on the brakes, but they wouldn't hold and the lorry ran backwards with six cows on board; it was touch and go if I stayed on the wheels or cocked to. But luckily it was early in the morning and there were no other vehicles on the road, so I managed to roll round into the car park. Then we got another lorry to back up and take the animals off.

Once I was bringing some animals home in the dusk, just up the road here, when I saw this car comin' straight towards me on my side of the road. I mowed down twelve yard of hedge tryin' to get out the way, but the car still hit me. It was this local woman who was nearly blind drivin' the car. She was only injured but her little girl was thrown out and killed. There was nothing I could do and I was cleared of all blame. Why she took that chance we'll never know.'

[On another occasion Harry had trouble with a big bull:] When I loaded this bull on the lorry I tied him up as usual, but when I stopped at another farm to collect a cow and dropped the back door I saw that he was loose. Immediately I tried to grab the rope, and shouted at the farmer not to let the cow out. But it was too late. The bull saw her and charged down the gate, which fell on me. But luckily for me he then jumped right over the fallen gate, else I wouldn't be here to tell the tale.

That was just one of several narrow squeaks. It's especially dangerous with bulls in a little wagon because as soon as you drop the door they're on top of you. With a bigger vehicle you have a little time to do something about it if a beast is loose. But I've never been afraid to tackle anything. If anyone 'ad a mad cow or a kicking horse they'd always say: 'Send for Harry, he'll shift it'.

Not surprisingly, Harry has been hurt many times. His worst injury was sustained when working for Trafford. 'One of his stallions had cut its leg very badly and I'd been dressing it for about a fortnight. Then one day when I bent down it lashed out for no apparent reason. Perhaps I'd touched a tender spot. Anyway, it kicked me 'ard and broke a blood vessel just above my eye so that the blood came out like a tap. It also broke both sets of me false teeth.' Harry then explained why he had entirely false teeth at the young age of twenty-six:

I never 'ad a good tooth in me life. It ran in the family. Eventually, when I was nineteen I 'ad toothache so bad that when I rode a bike I 'ad to cup one hand over me mouth to stop the air rushin' in. By then I'd 'ad enough so I went to the dentist at Tutbury, Mr Hunter, and said, 'You can take 'em all out!' He said: 'Why all of them?' I said: 'Because if me dad finds out I've been, he won't let me come again.' So I talked him into it, and I was determined to see it through, even though it hurt like hell with three abscesses under the teeth.

Another very bad time I 'ad was the result of rabbiting. I'd put in a line ferret in a warren under some pine trees, and when I was fumblin' about for the line in a hole I got a pine needle under my nail. Then I got blood poisoning in the thumb, and they cut the nail back three times, but it didn't get much better and in the end it didn't look much like a thumb.

Then one day I was loadin' hay in the rickyard when I hit that thumb and passed out with the pain on top of a stack, where I couldn't be seen from the ground. Lucky for me Betty Trafford came out and went into the hayloft, where she looked down and saw me. Next thing I knew I woke up in Derby hospital. Now I'm left with this deformed thumb.

Sometimes it was Harry's animals which came to grief:

Once I was carryin' this big fat sheep which collapsed in the back of the lorry and suffocated under the others. Another time I had five lambs killed. I'd only just moved them from one field to another, which I rented, when lightning struck this beech tree which fell on 'em. I found them when I next went up to feed.

The beech is a very unpredictable tree. Once I was talkin' to this farmer and his wife when this big beech branch snapped off for no reason and missed her nose by a whisker.

Because of the considerable expense, Harry has never been one for calling in the vet. 'It has to be a real emergency, with what they charge. Even if you 'ave an animal with a broken leg you're better off takin' it to the slaughterhouse.'

Harry's greatest cure-all, for both himself and his animals, is a mixture of goose grease and vinegar which he keeps in a large jar wrapped in a polythene bag, and which does not smell anything like as bad as I expected. He prepares this himself when he kills a goose at Christmas or on some other special occasion. 'It's my favourite for soothing lumps and aches and pains.

'Another good thing is old motor oil mixed with flowers of sulphur. I use this to cure sweetage [sweet-itch], when a horse rubs itself red raw in the mane and tail and along the back.

'A lot of horses get "fever in the feet", when the sole of the foot drops down and touches the floor where it shouldn't do. For that I keep paintin' on pure turpentine until it improves.'

There must be something in all these old remedies because Harry is one of the most youthful-looking octogenarians I have ever met, despite having had a very serious kidney disease in his late sixties, when they 'wrote him off'. He has always cut a dash with the ladies, and still goes to dances regularly. Quite recently, after a turn around the floor, his partner said to him: 'Oooh! That was like stepping out of a Sierra into a Rolls Royce! My husband is so stiff!' Once Harry even won a ploughing match for being the best looking. 'It was just over the field there and I won a prize even though I 'adn't 'ad a plough in me 'ands for two years. There was the boss's daughter and another girl judgin' and I think they must 'ave seen me with me shirt off!'

Another of Harry's sidelines is what he calls 'flitting': transporting people's furniture in his specially cleaned-out cattle lorry when they move house. Most of these jobs come through recommendation, and he has been as far as Inverness, London and Margate, to properties as difficult to access as the top floor of a block of flats.

Harry has never suffered fools gladly and has a particularly dislike of 'men with brass plates', those who seem more concerned with bureaucracy than getting a job done. Among the most reviled are some ministry men, especially those who handled the last foot and mouth outbreak in the area: 'They made a right muck of it, killing

Applying a mixture of goose grease and vinegar to soothe aches and pains

21

animals which should 'ave been spared and leaving others which should 'ave been put down. And when they burnt all the carcases over there, all the bits went up with the smoke and rained down on the cars passing along that road, taking goodness knows what all over the country.'

But despite his strong views on many subjects, it is Harry's tremendous sense of humour and air of contentment which stay with you. A widower for ten years, he has two daughters and one son and remains very popular among local farmers. There seems little doubt that the man often described as 'a law unto himself' will be dealing and driving till the day he runs out of goose grease.

LAWYER OF THE LAND

PAUL RYAN

SOLICITOR
County Laois, Ireland

When I drove into the old market-place at rural Rathdowney a funeral party was leaving the church. Among the mourners was 75-year-old solicitor Paul Ryan, although that was hardly surprising because, as his son Michael told me, 'It's not regarded as a good funeral unless Da's at it'. During some fifty-two years as a solicitor in his sleepy little home town, Paul has made innumerable friends, many through upholding rights in land.

'Land is at the base of Irish life: ownership gives you freedom', Paul told me with great conviction as we chatted by the fire at his comfortable Irish Midlands home. And, not surprisingly, he has acquired quite a few acres of his own along the way; though never with the intention merely to accumulate wealth. This humble man 'came from a world of self-sufficiency, and much of that has hung on'. The tireless hand which still interprets the law for 5½ days a week can milk a cow and draft a will with equal ease.

But it was a very different and relatively lawless Ireland in which Paul grew up. The country's battle for independence, from the Easter Rebellion of 1916, through the troubles of Sinn Fein, the Black and Tans, the Free State (1922), the Civil War (1922–3), to the loosening of official bonds achieved by Mr de Valera, affected countryman and townsman alike. Indeed, Paul's very earliest memories are of 'stragglers from the Civil War – soldiers – shooting mounds of pigeon and duck.

'Also in 1922, father was coming back with a keg of whiskey in his Ford Model T when he ran into a trench. The car was wrecked and the whiskey sprang out. He had to be pulled out by a local farmer's "hinny", a type of mule, bigger and stronger than a donkey but infertile.'

*'We poached, too. I tickled t'ousands
and t'ousands of trout…'*

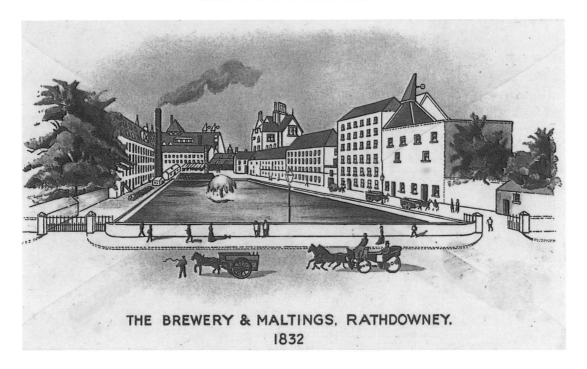

THE BREWERY & MALTINGS, RATHDOWNEY.
1832

The youngest of five children, Paul was christened Peter Paul, being born on 29 June 1918, 'the Feast of St Peter, which used to be a holy day'. And with four older sisters he was never spoiled by his farmer's son father, then a publican and grocer. Rural Ireland of the day was a little boy's paradise. 'Nobody minded where you went at all – it was all "free" ground.' Consequently, Paul indulged in all the usual country pastimes of the day. Here he recounts some childhood experiences:

Each evening after school we robbed birds' nests, but sometimes the egg would break in my mouth as I descended the tree.

We poached, too. I tickled t'ousands and t'ousands of trout – became rather an expert at it. The secret was to move the hand quietly under the bank, never rush and grab. We went down on our bikes to hunt rabbits with sticks – you'd see movement through the nettles, then wham! And I went out with the local postman killing hares and rabbits with two greyhounds and a terrier. And when we went fishing at night we took good care to avoid the guards.

And I used to keep birds; I had a pair of barn owls which a man gave me, and with limed twigs I caught goldfinches, linnets, blackbirds, thrushes and, worse still, a lark!

They were very hard times for many people. Almost every other house had a victim of TB (tuberculosis), and there was no cure. The area had lots of small farmers and small shops, though most are closed now. The town had four blacksmiths, four tailors, four bakers and cobblers, but now they've all gone. Most workers used to live in stone and mortar cabins with thatched roofs. There was a great deal of poverty and drinking: Rathdowney had seventeen pubs for a population of only a thousand, but they served a big hinterland. A small bottle of Guinness cost 6d and a pint of draught 9d.

The local brewery was Perry's, a very benevolent firm; no one was ever sacked. Their beer was brought out by horses and I bottled many a barrel by hand. In the autumn – mostly

September – the farmers brought big bags of barley on carts to the square, where they'd queue up with their horses before going in to have the corn tested. The brewery paid on the quality of grain. Prices were very high during World War I, but then fell, and many farmers went broke. Father bought a farm at Abbeyleix in 1925, but sold it during the economic war, in 1932. Many of my school mates and their families ended up going to America and England.

'… if you run it [poteen] through twice it's much better quality'

Of course, lots of poteen was made – and still is – illegally. It's a poison really, and the people who make it generally succumb to it because they're testing and tasting it all the time. Some people say it's only good for rubbing into a greyhound's back, but it has a certain mystique because it avoids the excise duty. It's made in every vicinity and socially it's not considered illegal, but the guards and clergy are very much down on it. Any stills discovered are destroyed, although now they are harder to detect because they use gas. In the old days they lit turf fires, which were easier to find.

I've defended people for making poteen several times, and there's very few years without a case. Last time I was in court I overdid it, defending a 'small' farmer on the edge of the bog. Unfortunately the judge, rather a wayward Justice, knew the truth, that the contestant was a substantial farmer, so he fined him the maximum, which was £500. The man's wife was in on the act, too.

Usually the police get tipped off; they are well acquainted with what's happening everywhere. It's said that when they make a seizure, if it's a particularly good batch, they keep some. It's mostly made with barley, sugar and yeast, and if you run it through twice it's much better quality and less dangerous.

During Paul's childhood bacon and cabbage was a favourite meal:

Father killed his own pigs and cured his own bacon. He had a licence from the British government and sent some to Pimms at Montmelick, for export, especially during the first war. And out here we had a little field which he had bought in 1918 to keep a few cattle in. He was very proud of it, and also grew flat Dutch cabbage; the average head weighed 30lb, but one was 43lb! We were organic to the nth degree, and had an ass and cart to fetch the dung; but once I overdid the dung and we had no cabbage because it all went to seed!

Almost every shopkeeper in town had his own patch of land on the outskirts of town, where he kept his own cow. And almost every working man kept a pig or two in the back yard. There was a particular logic in pig-keeping here, as you could buy 'grains' [barley which had been processed in beer-making] cheaply from the local brewery. That fattened the pigs all right.

With so many Ryans around, nicknames were often used to make identification easier. Not surprisingly, as Paul's father was closely involved with pig-killing, their branch of the family became known as the 'Sticker Ryans'. In contrast, those who wanted to copy their neighbour in having the latest flush loo at the end of the garden were dubbed the 'Proud Arse Ryans'.

Travelling was much harder then, and the roads were 'lethal for tyres and for the hooves of cattle. The county council employed men to break stones for the roads at half-a-crown per large box. Then a steam roller came along and pressed them in.'

As a boy, Paul often walked about eighteen miles with cattle from Thurles Fair. In his own words:

> I accompanied the paid drover. There were quite a few journeymen in those days, and they'd turn their hand to anything to earn a few bob. Sometimes beasts would break out and run off across the bog, and then we'd have to go all the way back for them next day because we couldn't leave the other cattle. Animals were sold in the town square starting at between five and six in the morning once a month, and the dealers came and bargained by hand. Most cattle would eventually end up in Dublin market, and buyers would come over from England. I always remember that in July 1934 beef was just 15s a hundredweight in Dublin market.
>
> If you had a bullock which was inclined to wander – a 'thiever' – you punched a hole in his ear, threaded a circle of woodbine [wild honeysuckle] through it, and tied it there. Legend was that it stopped the beast going through a gap in the hedge or trying to escape through the barn door when being slaughtered.

Back from America: three Rathdowney men (standing on cart) in March 1932

Father had no fear at all. Once he had a bull in a little shed with no crushes for handling the beast. Another time I saw him attacked by a bullock and the blood was running down his boot. I was terrified, but he didn't make anything of it at all. He'd get the beast by the nose with two fingers, and twist its neck to keep it still, a matter of brute strength and some skill. But people were tough in those days.

Farmers tended to cure their own sick animals then, and lots were brought to Father for various ailments, such as timber tongue, a fungus which caused cattle tongues to swell; Father provided potassium permanganate and beniodine of mercury for that.

Father was also a very strong believer in law and order, and a great admirer of the rule of law. He would not tolerate bad language. Mother was always praying

A wandering bullock had honeysuckle threaded through its ear

and Dad had strong morals, but he would not be dominated by any cleric! If any robber came in he would certainly be confronted. Dad had to use his fists several times.

There were lots of tinkers around then and they used to have huge rows and beat each other up. One day Terry O'Reilly, the king of the tinkers, came to our pub and knocked on the door. Father said: 'You've had enough – off you go'. But Terry swiped at Father, but missed, and Dad gave him a short left jab; the tinker fell in the channel, Dad sent for the police and Terry was taken to the barracks overnight. The poor fellow had a broken jaw which never set properly. But we felt sorry for him, and whenever he came round after that he was always given a free pint.

A much more serious incident occurred during the Civil War, in 1922:

A few men – one local – came into our snug at Ryan's Bar for a drink one day, their guns hanging out of their pockets for all to see. So father strode up and told them to put them away – he always liked to be the one in authority. Also, he sensed that there was a robbery in the offing, and that they were casing the joint.

That night, when Mother was asleep, Father, having said nothing to the family, tiptoed down and barricaded the front door. He had umpteen knives and cleavers for pig-killing, so he armed himself with a big one for cutting a pig's head in two, and sat by the back door, where he thought they might come if unsuccessful at the front. His intention was that the first one who came in wouldn't go back!

The hours passed, but nobody came. Then at 4am he heard a motor car, a very rare thing in town then. He looked out and saw a car go past the pub with one man on the running board half in the car and groaning. He discovered that the men had robbed the only bank in town, and that the manager had fired several shots at them from his upstairs window as they made off. Two robbers were injured and the one on the running board died of buckshot wounds to

The bank manager fired from his upstairs window as they made off

his back. The others buried him in the local bog and shared the loot. Their identities were pretty well known, but robberies were common then and they were never brought to justice. Law and order had more or less broken down at that stage.

Ironically, the bank manager's quarters, from which the shots were fired, are now the Ryans' solicitors' office, dispensing law by gentler means.

Between the ages of four and nine Paul attended the local convent school 'where the nuns were very kind', but from nine to fourteen he went to the local segregated national school 'which was really a school of punishment rather than learning. I bore several "lumps" of knowledge for years after. But that tyrant of a teacher did teach me advanced literature.'

A year later than usual, Paul went away to secondary school, boarding at Tipperary for five years. 'It was run by an order of priests – Holy Ghost fathers – and we worked hard and played hard, especially rugby [Paul captained the school team] and hurling. Anybody who wanted to work did well.' Modestly, Paul told me: 'I had a one-sided brain and still can't add two and two.' But few succeeded as he did, getting first place for French in Ireland in his leaving certificate and winning a scholarship to University College Dublin. 'The thing is, Irish parents came to place great emphasis on education because lots of them, including mine, only went to primary school. The generation before them didn't even get that.'

After gaining his BA in legal and political science, Paul took his MA in 1941. 'I thought I might as well carry on as I had four years' grant and the BA only took three years.' At the same time he continued his interest in rugby, at various times representing St Mary's College Dublin, UCD, Birr, Rathdowney and Carlow.

Despite his distinguished academic career, Paul was 'not a city person at all and was never tempted to work elsewhere'. So in 1943, after a daily cycle ride of twelve miles each way during his apprenticeship at Abbeyleix, he set up in practice in Rathdowney, in competition with one other solicitor. And with the threat of invasion by Germany, he joined the local defence force during World War II. 'We marched and drilled with World War I rifles, but it was all a waste of time.'

His first office was a service tenement adjacent to a butcher's stall, and in between reading Tolstoy's epic novel *War and Peace* (business was decidedly slow at first!) he might be asked to help winch up for butchering any animal killed during office hours. It was bad enough having to leave his desk to pull up a bullock on a rope, but whenever an inquisitive neighbour said: 'Any harm in asking you who that client was?' Paul would seethe at his curiosity. 'There was no demarcation between the professions in those days!'

Paul Ryan, graduate of University College, Dublin

30

Paul (centre of back row) in the St Mary's College rugby team 1938–39

Equally curious was the man who surreptitiously edged along the outside wall of the office until he could hear what was being said. Then there was the local schoolboy who was wont to jump up to peer into the window as he passed. One day Paul grabbed him, took him into the office and told him to have a good look around so that he would not have to jump up and down on the footpath any more. 'His curiosity was cured permanently.'

During his first ten years in practice Paul did not own a car; instead he visited farmers and other clients on his bike, 'a 28in Harp which cost £3 15s, complete with roadster tyres, pump and bell. It was stolen a few times but always came back. I was fit as a fiddle then, and would think nothing of a daily round trip of seventy to eighty miles to attend a hurling or football match.'

He has good reason to remember one day when he cycled out to make a will. 'It was 3 March 1948 and my wife-to-be, Katherine, was sitting in the garden as I went past. Her father was putting dung out for the potatoes in the kitchen garden, and that was the beginning of our romance. When we were married, in 1951, we lived in a few rooms over the office. You didn't go into debt in those days – it was all a gradual process.'

Paul has certainly met some eccentric and remarkable people on his travels. 'Once I went to this hill farm and there was a donkey in the kitchen; the owner lived alone and every night he took the animal in for company. Another old client was what we call a very "hard" character. When I went to see him he was in bed with his boots on, and the

'…and many a trout has been left by the front door'

bottle had fallen out of his hand onto the floor. Then there was the cross old lady whom we persuaded to put her cash in the bank, rather than the bedroom. When they counted out all the old £20 notes she declared: "Don't mix that money with anyone else's!".'

Notables, too, have needed Paul's expertise. 'In the old days I defended some very well known people for speeding, and none of them paid a fee.'

Yet Paul's establishment of a successful Midlands practice has not been without real excitement. 'During my time I've done with every type of hate, envy and pride – it's unbelievable.

'I've defended several murders – by stabbing and shooting, and a throat cut by a bottle in a pub row. Murder has even been committed over turf banks: if one man encroached on another's peat bog there'd be very bad blood about it. But I always try to discourage litigation because the only certainty of the outcome is the expense.

'One man I defended for shooting a trespasser was granted legal aid, and there was very little return for me. During the trial I took the relatives to Dublin each day, and afterwards they gave me a pair of ducks each Christmas to show their gratitude.' Some clients still bring turkeys at Christmas, and many an eel or trout has been left by the front door in recognition of services rendered. And neither Paul nor his son Michael, with whom he is now in partnership, ever needs to buy potatoes.

Modestly, Paul insists that what he did for some of these families was insignificant, 'but I can never repay the compliment. It's very rewarding to help, say, a small farmer for little return: it makes your day. After so long in a country practice you get to know everyone. Every man is a creature of habit, and you have your own special associations with a place.' But there can be few places which have benefited from the extraordinarily long devotion of one man to the extent that Rathdowney has through Paul Ryan. Were there more such lawyers of the land, far fewer people would say that real community spirit is long dead.

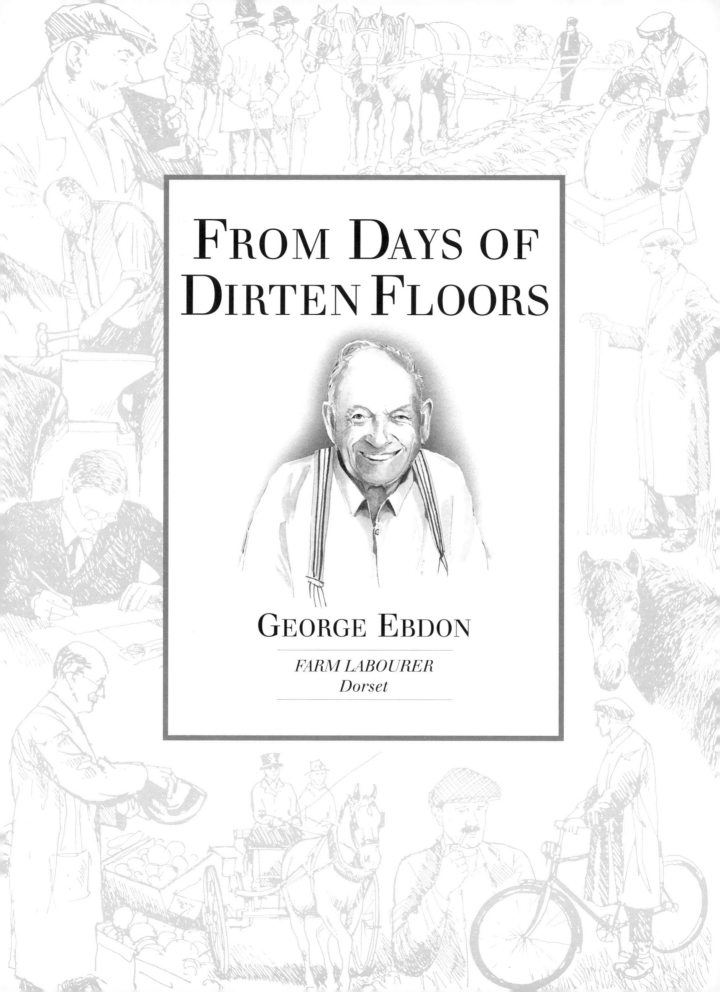

FROM DAYS OF DIRTEN FLOORS

GEORGE EBDON

FARM LABOURER
Dorset

When 97-year-old George Ebdon was a boy in deepest Dorset, living conditions were very different from those of today. In his own words:

The inside walls of our cottage were whitewashed with lime and water, the kitchen floor was big flagstones and the backhouse, where fuel, potatoes and other things were stored, had a dirten floor. But the earth was real hard where people walked on it, so Mother could brush up the crumbs just like on the stones.

The edge of the hearth stones was whitened with wet chalk – that was an everyday job for Mother. She cooked over the open fire, in a big boiling pot on a chain hanging from a crook in the chimney. Our lighting was mainly candles, but later we had paraffin lamps, and our fuel mostly sticks gathered on the farm as we couldn't afford much coal. The ol' toilet was the usual bucket in the garden; you emptied the contents on the vegetable land when it was full, and dug 'em in. It made wonderful cabbage and other crops, but that manure was in the ground a twelve-month before you grew on it.

But we were better off than a lot of people as we had water runnin' from a pipe all the time. It came from a spring and you'd take a bucket out and just catch it up. Most houses had wells, and lots had all dirten floors and some stonen staircases.

Born at Askerswell – 'just over the hill' – on 17 October 1898, George had two sisters and four brothers, three of whom 'went away to America to die'. His father was a farm worker, and his paternal grandfather a stonemason and chapel preacher. George's earliest memory is of Bonfire Night:

We young boys used to go on top the hills burnin' the fuzz [furze or gorse], which we set light to with special bonfire matches, like ordinary ones but longer. The farmer would come out and chase us off, but we only went some-where else.

'. . . we had water runnin' from a pipe all the time.'

Another thing we did was go in a farmer's field, get a mangold, cut the inside out, make a face and put a candle in it. Other times we'd play ring-o'-roses or marbles, which cost a penny for twelve. And we'd collect birds' eggs. There was nothin' else to do then – you 'ad to amuse yourself.

When I come older I went to work – at age eleven – as 'back-door boy', waiting on the farmer's wife, carryin' coal and sticks, cleanin' shoes and things for sixpence a week. But I still lived at home. Later the farmer put me on milkin' by hand, and as I got older still he sent me out in the fields ploughing.

There were about sixty children, big and small, at Askerswell school in they days, and they was supposed to go to fourteen. But the schoolmistress was related to some of the farmers and if they wanted you she'd let you go early. When the inspectors came round she used to mark us present in the book.

At the age of fourteen George worked full-time as a carter, from 6am to 6pm each day for one shilling a week. He describes his work:

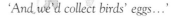

'And we'd collect birds' eggs…'

> With two horses I worked a WDG plough, made in Dorchester. I cut the corn with a binder, gathered the sheaves, and made and thatched ricks. Barley, oats and wheat were the main crops.
>
> I loved them Shire horses; faithful they was, and it was marvellous what they did. I got up at four o'clock in the morning to feed 'em with oats and chaff [chopped hay and straw]. On the farm we had six working horses plus unbroken two-year-olds runnin' in the field.
>
> We'd take our lunch at ten o'clock. Nosebags with oats and that went on the horses, and we used to sit on the plough and have bread and cheese or whatever Mother could afford. After half an hour it was back to work, and we returned to the yard at two o'clock as the horses had then done their day's work. Then we had one hour for dinner, and at three o'clock it was in the stable, cleaning out, washin' the horses down and puttin' in the bedding what they'd lie in by night. At six o'clock I'd go back in the house, but I'd come again at eight and rack up – feed the horses and see 'em right for the night.

The Ebdons bought little meat: 'The nearest butcher was about two miles away, and in any case the roads was all rough stones then. We mostly 'ad pies made from rabbits, which we caught in snares. Many times we just 'ad bread and butter and half an egg each. Mother

George playing the accordion at the age of ninety-six

would also cut a bloater in half. We couldn't afford more.' Sometimes George joined other villagers to fish for mackerel:

There were five boats down here on the beach, and a gang of about a dozen on each. We'd 'ave a fifty-yard seine net with men on each side, and pull the ropes in gradually, trapping the fish in a bag at the back. Most days we'd bring 'ome a dozen each, and on the way we'd sell some to anyone we met and get enough for half a pint of beer at the pub.

The first drink I 'ad was at the Swyre Bull, which was an ol' thatched place in they days. Everyone used to sit round a room with a stonen floor and no counter, mostly talkin' about work. The beer was Groves' and Palmer's from Weymouth and was very nice. When you wanted some, the landlord fetched it up from the cellar in waren [pottery] pint mugs and give 'e. The pub was open all day them days – you could 'ave a pint of beer at six in the mornin' if you wanted to. You could also buy a bit of bread and cheese, Cheddar or Dorset Blue, and pickled onions.

Sometimes in the Bull we'd play rings. You'd stand back and throw 'em over crooks on a board on the wall, with numbers on it. And we'd play shove-'a' penny. Darts came on later and done them games out; 'twas all dartin' then.

But we always enjoyed a good ol' sing-song. Some had mouthorgans to play, and I always liked in-and-outers [accordions]. I sent away to Germany for this Höhner over forty years ago. And even before we had the ol' gramophone with the big horn, we had a Zonophone.

During World War I, George was called up into the Royal Warwickshires:

T'wa'n't no option. They was so many bein' killed they sen' 'e to whatever regiment wanted 'e the most.

I trained in Northumberland, two or three miles from Blyth, and in 1917 went to France, in the trenches. I saw hundreds – no, thousands – of men and horses dead, all lying on top of each other. It's too bad to talk about. And if the guns didn't get you, then disease did. A lot of the boys who had the 'flu just lay in the trenches and died.

I was on the Somme on 21 March 1918, when the Germans made a big push and blowed we all to hell. That's when I got a bullet through the arm – see that mark? And I had shrapnel in there – just below my eye. It was at night when I was on guard duty at a dug-out just behind the front line. I was up top when a shell pitched near I and blowed I right up in the air and down again. Then they bullets was flyin' around. If you put your finger up or a bit of paper there'd soon be a ping as the German snipers tried to pick it off.

I suppose I was lucky. I was in hospital in Belgium for a month and they took most of the shrapnel out. The bullet went straight through my forearm, and at night, when the nurses had gone quiet, I used to put a penny in the wound to keep it all festery, so they'd keep me in a bit longer and I wouldn't 'ave to go back to the front. We all did it. But after hospital it was straight back into the mud and water again; and then I was lightly gassed.

After Armistice Day, on 11 November 1918, George arrived at a rest area. 'There were these big bottles of rum there, and as we were very happy we got very drunk, but the officers didn't say nothing. I suppose it was because of what we'd been through.'

When he went back home on leave George discovered that his former employer at Chilcombe needed him back on the farm. 'He wrote to the War Office, and just one day after I got back to France the corporal said I was wanted, but I couldn't think I'd done anythin' wrong. I was told to go back to England right away.'

After a while the euphoria of being home subsided and George began to miss his army companions. He even contemplated joining up again. 'It was touch and go.' But he soon settled into the old routine and remained at Samways, Chilcombe for some five years.

The pace of Dorset country life had scarcely changed, so people like George still regularly walked long distances. When courting in the early 1920s he lived at Gorwell, Little Bredy, and frequently walked to Swyre to collect his future wife, Clara, to take her

During World War I George served in the Royal Warwickshires

Michael Ebdon with old horse bells once used by his father, George

to a dance at Abbotsbury. Afterwards they would walk back to Swyre, where George would have a cup of tea before walking back to Gorwell, 'and all that was after a full day working on the farm, mind!'

During World War II George and Clara had two evacuee girls at their Swyre cottage. 'We were offered two boys or two girls, but we said "no" to the boys as we had two already, so the boys went next door. Later on we had two more girls to stay.' Then George was a corporal in the Home Guard, at which time he was at Berwick Farm; here he spent the last forty years of his working life, continuing full-time until the age of seventy-five. 'Then I automatically had to draw the old-age pension, so I went part-time.'

Over the years George did 'all there is in farm work', and was a very familiar figure in his hobnail boots, corduroy trousers and blue slop jacket, round and about the fields and twisting lanes of south Dorset; he even made cider for the farm workers. 'We had this press with a wheel on top, and I would layer it up with wheaten straw between the apples, always tucking the ends in till it was about two to three feet high; this stack was called a cheese. There were fourteen of us on the farm, and each man drew a quart of cider in the morning.'

Although George's 1911 Swyre cottage is still much as it was when he went there in 1933, and he still lives in a relatively unspoilt corner of Dorset, he has seen many significant changes in village life. 'In the old days if you could 'ave got in on the Swyre to live, you was quids in. All this estate used to be the Duke of Bedford's, and I rented this place. Then the ol' duke died about thirty years ago and everythin' was sold up to pay death duties. Us sitting tenants were given first option, and I just had enough to buy it; the price was only in the hundreds. But after the houses were sold off people only lived here a short time, and soon you knew nobody. It's mostly all strangers now. People can be friendly, saying good mornin' and all that, without bein' neighbourly. In the ol' days we was always goin' to see each other, havin' cups of tea.'

Clara died in 1974, but George still has the bachelor company of one of his two sons, Michael, who recently retired after forty years as a Dorset roadman. Together they maintain a large garden, well stocked with fine vegetables, many of which they give to friends. Others are preserved in much the same way as when George was a boy and there were no refrigerators; runner beans, for example, are chopped up small, well salted and put into large jars. 'No water is added,' says George. 'All that you can see in the jar is drawn out by the salt. They'll keep all year like that.'

George, who has never owned a car or a telephone, is also a good cook and is renowned for his apple dumplings. 'I likes my pastry,' he told me. 'I'm gonna 'ave a dumpling today and I 'ad one last night for tea.' With such an appetite for life, it's little wonder that George remains so fit.

Of Taking Small Birds with Lime

Your Lime-bush must be a main bough of any bushy tree, as Birch or Willow, or for want of them, Sallow, Poplar, or Aspen; whose twigs are long, smooth, and streight, without pricks, knots, or any other roughness or crookedness; having pickt and trim'd it (yet not taking away any of the little bud-knots) lime every twig and branch from the top down within four fingers or there-about of the bottom. The body and main branches must not be touched with any Lime at all. Dabble not on your lime too thick, nor yet let any part be left bare, or want its proportion, that ought to be limed.

Your Bush thus prepared, carry it forth into the fields where the haunts of the small birds are; and place it as near as you can to any of these haunts, if it be a hedge or tree close to them, etc, provided that where-ever you pitch it down, you may very near it have some close Covert to lie concealed in, and there chirp like a sparrow, or call with a note like the Linnet or Bull-finch (as the Cocks use to do when they miss the Hens, or the Hens the Cocks) altering your note according to your fancy, but continually calling in one note or other. This Art and Ability is gotten by diligent observing the Birds notes abroad, and by practice. But if you cannot frame your mouth to these sounds, get you a Bird-call; and having learnt how to use it Artificially, you shall sit in your Covert, and call the Birds to you: And when you see any of them light upon your Bush let them alone, and move not till you see them safely entangled, which their own skipping up and down, and struggling when they find themselves snared, will do better than any affright from you whatsoever: Neither shall you stir for a single Bird or two, but stay till many be entangled: For the first that are taken with their striving and fluttering in the Bush be as good as Stales, and make a world of others repair to them, which you may then take: And this exercise you may continue from before Sun-rise till ten of the Clock in the Fore-noon, and from one in the Afternoon till almost Sun-set in the evening.

If you want a Call you may make use of a Stale; as of a Bat or two, placed next to your Lime-bush in such apparent manner that no bird thereabouts but may behold them; which will no sooner be perceived, but every bird will come to gaze and wonder at them: Then having no other convenient lighting place but the Lime-bush, they will flock as thick into the same as may be, and so you may take them at pleasure. So the Owl may in like manner be employed, which by reason she is more melancholy and less stirring than the Bat, and also of greater bulk, and sooner perceived, is a better Stale than the Bat. For want of a live Owl or Bat the skin of either stuft, or an artificial Owl made of wood and painted may serve the turn.

The Ornithology of Francis Willughby, 1678

Country Characters

It would not be possible to enumerate all the characters you are likely to meet on your rambles. With many of them you will form an acquaintance almost too readily. The mole-catcher, the rabbit-catcher, the rat-catcher, for example, pursue avocations with which a boy almost always likes to make some acquaintance. But some that you are inclined to pass as uninteresting will perhaps furnish most entertainment in the end. I know a frail old fellow who earns a poor livelihood by breaking metal on the roadside, who can keep one amused for hours together with his conversation. And the more you know concerning open-air life, the more will you like to listen to those who know about it and know little else.

P. Anderson Graham,
Country Pastimes for Boys, 1895

To Sweeten the Church

In the 'Herball to the Bible', 1587, mention is made of 'sedges and rushes, the whiche manie in the countrie doe use in summer-time to strewe their parlors or churches, as well for coolness as for pleasant smell'. The species preferred was the *Calamus aromaticus*, which, when bruised, gives forth an odour resembling that of the myrtle; in the absence of this, inferior kinds were used. Provision was made for strewing the earthen or paved floors of churches with straw or rushes, according to the season of the year.

The Rev G. Miles Cooper observes: 'Though few are ignorant of this ancient custom it may not perhaps be so generally known, that the strewing of churches grew into a religious festival, dressed up into all that picturesque circumstance where-with the old church well knew how to array its ritual.

Remains of it linger to this day in remote parts of England. In Westmoreland, Lancashire, and districts of Yorkshire, there is still celebrated between hay-making and harvest a village fete called the rush-bearing. Young women dressed in white, and carrying garlands of flowers and rushes, walk in procession to the parish church, accompanied by a crowd of rustics, with flags flying and music playing. There they suspend their floral chaplets on the chancel rails, and the day is concluded with a simple feast.

Chambers' *Book of Days*, 1866

Haunt of the British Tyger

I have been assured that in the county of Northampton, in the forests of Rockingham and Whittlebury, there remains, at this day, sufficient timber to build the navy of England twice over; and as canals are now forming in those parts, it may soon be an easy matter to convey it from its deep recesses to any of the King's yards. These forests also, particularly Whittlebury, are infested by the wild-cat; which the naturalists call the British tyger.

William Gilpin, *Remarks on Forest Scenery*, 1794

Bandit Country

In Buckinghamshire we have the forests of Bernwood and Clitern. Bernwood runs along the hilly country from Aylesbury almost to Oxford. Clitern was formerly a very thick impervious wood, and noted for being the haunt of banditti, who long infested the country; till a public-spirited abbot of St Alban's broke their confederacy, by bringing many of them to justice, and destroying their retreats.

William Gilpin, *Remarks on Forest Scenery*, 1794

To Shoot Snipe by Night

Hang the lantern by a broad leathern belt, over a man's neck, and strap it round his body, to keep it steady. Let the man carry a very large, deep-sounding bell, such as is hung round the necks of cows, in each hand, and keep incessantly ringing them: this will prevent the noise of your feet disturbing the animals you are searching after. Proceed to the springs, and other places which are not frozen up in the hard weather: there, at night, you will be sure to find both wild fowl and snipes. Walk behind the man carrying the lantern, with a double gun; one

barrel loaded with duck-shot, the other with snipe-shot. This amusement was called, one hundred years ago, the bell and muffet; and my father told me, when he was a young man, it was much practised.

Colonel George Hanger, *To All Sportsmen*, 1814

The Southdown Shepherd

One old shepherd, an ancient of the ancients, grey and bent, has spent so many years among his sheep that he has lost all notice and observation – there is no 'speculation in his eye' for anything but his sheep. In his blue smock frock, with his brown umbrella, which he has had no time or thought to open, he stands listening, all intent, to the conversation of the gentlemen who are examining his pens. He leads a young restless collie by a chain; the links are polished to a silvery brightness by continual motion; and the collie cannot keep still; now he runs one side, now the other, bumping the old man, who is unconscious of everything but the sheep.

Richard Jefferies, *Nature Near London*, 1893

Hooking Sea-Gulls

On a spring day there is a peculiar pleasure in walking up and down the fields with a plough-man as he holds the stilts of his plough, with which he and his team are breaking up the soil. And let me tell you there is no healthier odour than the smell of fresh upturned earth, and no sight more pleasing than that of the sturdy labourer and his team followed by a cloud of black rooks and white sea-gulls. Cruel boys sometimes catch the latter by setting a fish-hook baited with a worm in the furrow; the rook cannot be taken in that way, for it tears the worm to bits before eating it.

P. Anderson Graham, *Country Pastimes for Boys*, 1895

Champagne Stimulant

The best stimulant for persons who have been exposed to cold is champagne. It acts more quickly than brandy or whisky. If a more powerful effect is wanted, brandy and champagne should be taken alternately; but this remedy should never be used except by persons suffering from a shock. Champagne is our drink when we go wildfowling, and we find that nothing is so good for recuperating.

The Shooting Times, 8 April 1887

Blackberrying

The blackberry is the king of fruits and gathering it is one of the most delightful pastimes of the year. Some poor people gather blackberries either to sell, or to preserve and make dumplings with in winter, and when this is the case, those who gather merely for pleasure, ought to avoid the near and easily accessible places. Besides, if the pickers are numerous, they carry off all the best, and are not in any way particular about whether they overload their baskets with inferior fruit or not. And yet they often display a curious lack of ingenuity, or a great reluctance to take a little trouble. One autumn in Hampshire I was greatly amused by an industrious old man, who was an exception to the general rule. Low down there was nothing but red, undeveloped, half-ripe fruit, no one thought it worth while to pick; up above were myriads of deliciously ripe and beautiful berries. The old man had thought of this, and carried with him a small, light ladder, which he took first to one side, and then the other, exciting general envy as he filled his vessel with choice blackberries.

P. Anderson Graham,
Country Pastimes for Boys, 1895

Home-Made Rods and Lines

Many of the fathers and grandfathers of the young fishermen of to-day used rods that were made by some village mechanic, often the carpenter or wheelwright. Occasionally, someone whose ordinary labour was very different had a genius for this work. I remember a schoolmaster who turned out an excellent article. It used to be made in three pieces, the bottom of ash, the middle of hickory, the top of lancewood. Should there be anyone in your neighbourhood who can make rods, you will hardly do better than apply to him. But such a variety of good rods is now sold cheaply by the dealer that the village rod-makers receive little encouragement.

For very coarse fishing any line will do if it be strong enough. Many a large jack or good basket of eels has been pulled out with a fine whip-cord. In the

winter evenings you may make a capital hair line for yourself. Hairs are easily obtained in the country, and all the apparatus needed consists of three sticks about three inches long. With your pocket knife the end of each may be split, and a strand of hair inserted in each cleft. Plait these together, feeding each with a new hair whenever there is one run out. Six hairs will make a stout line, and by diminishing the number or using two sticks instead of three it may be made as fine as desired. Home-made articles are not in as much request now as they used to be, and probably rather than take the trouble you will go to the shop, where, for about half-a-crown, you may obtain forty or fifty yards of line, made of undressed silk. Many lines are sold at a cheaper rate, but very low-priced lines are anything but a saving in the end.

P. Anderson Graham,
Country Pastimes for Boys, 1895

Fieldsports and the Great War

Owing to the terrible war that has opened in Europe it is safe to presume life will be a dull and dreary affair in the country this forthcoming winter. Already several naval and military men have sent word to their head gamekeepers cancelling their shooting arrangements, and intimating that they are prepared to let the shoots if tenants can be found, which is doubtful. Many hunting men, too, are backing out of the arrangements they were entering into to rent hunting-boxes, and are holding their horses in readiness for the Army, in the event of their being needed. In the light of the present events, poaching, of course, will be an everyday occurrence, and the gamekeepers will be powerless to hold the offendors in check. On most estates the game will be shot by the keepers with the help of farmers, and distributed among the surrounding poor. No shooting man with any feeling for his fellow-being will allow the game to leave the district in which it has been reared. With meat at famine prices, there is certain to be a very large demand for ferrets for rabbiting purposes. A naval officer has telegraphed to his kennelman that as our navy has become entangled in the conflict the whole of his kennel of 20-odd gundogs are to be destroyed instantly. For a time there will be a large demand for dogs as guards, and those who have terriers, mastiffs and other dogs suitable for guarding property.

The Shooting Times, 8 August 1914

New Forest Horses

A diminutive breed of horses runs wild in New-forest. In general however the horse is private property; tho sometimes with difficulty ascertained. Numbers of people, who have lands in the neighbourhood of the forest, have a right of commoning in it; and most of the cottagers, who border on it, assume that right. Many of them have two or three mares; and some, who make it their business to breed colts, have droves.

Prickly Diet
Herds of twenty, or thirty are often seen feeding together; in summer especially, when they have plenty of pasturage, and can live as they please. In winter they are obliged to separate, and seek their food, as they can find it. In general indeed they are left, in all seasons, to take their chance in the forest. Where there is no expense, there can be no great loss; and what is saved, is so much gained. In marshy parts a severe winter often goes hardly with them. But in dry grounds, where heath and furze abound, they pick up a tolerable winter-subsistence; especially if they have learned the little arts of living, which necessity teaches. Of these arts, one of the most useful is to bruise, and pound with their fore-feet, the prickly tops of furze. This operation, which I have often seen performed, prepares the rigid diet of a furze-bush in some degree for mastication; and renders it rather less offensive to the palate. From

observing perhaps this instinct in a horse, furze is sometimes pounded in a mill, where fodder is scarce; and affords a wholesome nutriment for horses.

Colt Catching
When such colts, as have long run wild, are to be caught for sale, their ideas of liberty are so unconfined, from pasturing in so wild a range, that it is matter of no little difficulty to take them. Sometimes they are caught by slight of hand, with a rope and a noose. But if this method fail, they are commonly hunted down by horse-men, who relieve each other. Colt-hunting is a commone practice in the forest. The colts which feed on Obergreen, are sometimes taken by the following strategem. In this part runs a long bog, described under the name of Long-slade-bottom; which is crossed by a mole, thrown over it. With this passage the colt is well acquainted; and on being pursued, is easily driven towards it. When he is about the middle of the mole, two or three men start up in front, and oblige him to leap into the bog, where he is intangled, and seized.

Barbarous Practices
Within this century, I believe, the barbarous custom of docking horses came in use; and hath passed through various modifications, like all other customs, which are not founded in nature, and truth. A few years ago the *short* dock was the only *tail* (if it may be called such) in fashion, both in the army, and in carriages. The absurdity however of this total amputation began to appear. The gentlemen of the army led the way. They acknowledged the beauty, and use of the tail, as nature made it. The *short* dock every where disappeared; and all dragoon-horses now parade with long tails.

The *nag-tail* however still continued in use. Of this there are several species, all more or less mutilated. The most unnatural is the *nicked-tail*; so named from a cruel operation used in forming it. The under sinews of the dock being divided, the tail starts upwards, directly contrary to the position, which nature intended. The nag-tail is still seen in all genteel carriages. Nor will any person of fashion ride a horse without one. Even the gentlemen of the army, who have shewn the most sense in the affair of horse-tails, have been so misled, as to introduce the nag-tail into the light dragoons.

The same absurd notions, which have led men to cut off the tails of horses, have led them also to cut off their ears. I speak not of low grooms, and jockies; we have lately seen the studs of men of the first fashion, misled probably by grooms, and jockies, producing only cropt-horses.

When a horse has wide, lopping ears, as he sometimes has, without spring, or motion in them; a man may be tempted to remove the deformity. But to cut a pair of *fine ears* out of the head of a horse, is, if possible, a still greater absurdity, than to cut off his tail. Nothing can be alledged in its defence. The ear neither retards motion; nor flings dirt.

With regard to the *utility* of the ear, it is not improbable, that cropping it may injure the horse's hearing: there is certainly less concave surface to receive the vibrations of the air. I have heard it also asserted that this mutilation injures his health: for when a horse has lost that pent-house, which nature has given him over his ear, it is reasonable to believe that wind, and rain may get in, and give him cold. Hail, I have been told, is particularly injurious to him.

William Gilpin,
Remarks on Forest Scenery, 1794

Deplorable Maniac

Not finding Colonel Mitford at home, we took a ramble into his woods at Exbury, in Hampshire. Among these unknown woods our way at length became perplexed; and the sun was now set. Having no time therefore to lose, we inquired at a lonely cottage, which we found in a sheltered glade. Nothing could indicate peace and happiness more, than this little sheltered spot; and we expected to find a neat, peaceful, contented family within. But we found that a happy scene will not always make happy inhabitants. At the door stood two, or three squalid children with eager, famished countenances staring through matted hair. On entering the hovel, it was so dark that we could at first see nothing. By degrees a scene of misery opened. We saw other ragged children within; and were soon struck with a female figure, groveling at full length by the side of a few embers, upon the hearth. Her arms were naked to her shoulders; and her rags scarcely covered her body. On our speaking to her, she uttered in return a mixture of obscenity, and imprecations. We had never seen so deplorable a maniac.

We had not observed, when we entered, what now struck us, a man sitting in a corner of the hovel, with his arms folded, and a look of dejection, as is lost in despair. We asked him, Who that wretched person was? She is my wife, said he, with a composed melancholy; and the mother of these children. He seemed to be a man of great sensibility; and it struck us, what distress he must feel, every evening, after his labour, when, instead of finding a little domestic comfort, he met the misery, and horror of such a house – the total neglect of his little affairs – his family without any overseer, brought up in idleness, and dirt – and his wife, for whom he had no means of providing either assistance, or cure, lying so wretched an object always before him.

On relating our adventure at supper, we were informed, that the man, whose appearance of sensibility had affected us so much, was one of the most hardened, mischievous fellows in the country – that he had been detected in sheep-stealing – that he had killed a neighbour's horse in an act of revenge – and that it was supposed, he had given his wife, who was infamous likewise, a blow in a quarrel, which had occasioned her malady.

William Gilpin,
Remarks on Forest Scenery, 1794

Only ''Am an' Eggs'

On his travels along the Wye, from Ross to Chepstow, Louis Jennings asked: 'Can anyone tell me why it is that at all these hotels only two or three things fit to be eaten are known to the landlords? For breakfast you are invariably offered "'am an' eggs", while for dinner in this region the *menu* is never altered – "hox-tail, sole, and a cutlet". The waiter has no suggestions – he runs off his old list glibly, fidgets the spoons about, gives his dirty necktie a twist, and then stands smiling vacantly. "Steak or chop?", you *must* want one of those? No? – then try the cold meat; or come now, what do you say to some briled 'am? Not like that either? The waiter, who smells horribly of brandy-and-water, and has a parlous red face, begins to look upon you askance, as a very objectionable person. Evidently a "gent as is hard to please". Will you have some poached heggs? Last week there were some kidneys in the house, but they are all gone. Perhaps it is quite as well that they are. The visitor, feeling rather rueful, mildly suggests salmon. You might as well ask for the moon. And yet there are at least two rivers not far off in which the finest flavoured salmon in the world is caught. But you stand a better chance of getting a Severn salmon in Bond Street than you do at Chepstow or Gloucester.'

Louis Jennings,
Field Paths and Green Lanes, 1878

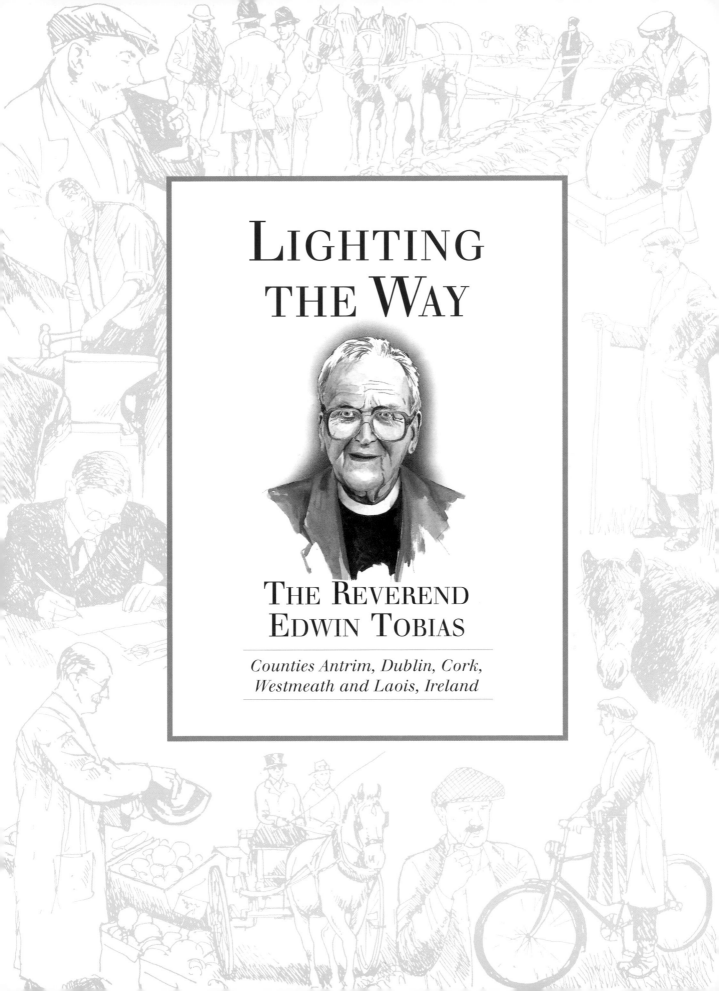

LIGHTING THE WAY

THE REVEREND EDWIN TOBIAS

Counties Antrim, Dublin, Cork,
Westmeath and Laois, Ireland

The sadness which surrounds a disused country church often bears false witness to the great devotion of past parishioners. Rarely has this been more true than in the west Cork parish where Edwin Tobias was rector in the early 1950s. He has vivid recollections of this.

The main church was in the village of Timoleague, where, during the seasons of Advent and Lent, I had mid-week services. One of my outlying churches stood on high ground and served a small number of very devoted people. After service one Sunday during Advent, I was asked if it would be possible to have mid-week services there, too. I said: 'Yes, of course, but there are no lights in the church'; only to be told: 'Leave that to us, sir!'

A date was fixed, but when I arrived on my bicycle I found the church in darkness. As I waited I began to wonder if I had mistaken the day. Then, looking down over the valley, I saw lights dotted here and there, and somehow they all seemed to be converging on the church. As they drew close my heart warmed as I realised that each member of the congregation was carrying a storm lantern, which they hung up in the church. By the same light by which they milked the cows at home, we worshipped God that evening, as we prepared ourselves for His coming.

These people were so loyal I arranged for the bishop to visit them. When I took him to the chosen house for tea, we found that the people had painted the whole building, from top to bottom, inside and out, and had even bought new furniture specially for the occasion!

Afterwards, as we sat in the car, the bishop paused for a minute and said: 'It's very humbling'. The worst of it is that the church is closed now.

Edwin with his parents in about 1919

The Minister
Solemn and Workmanlike

This prophetic card was sent to 4-year-old Edwin from Blackburn on 24 September 1920. On it is written '...a picture of you in years to come. Love to mother. Uncle B '

But just as those lanterns lit the path to peace, Edwin Tobias himself has been among the brightest of guiding lights during over half a century in holy orders, mostly ministering to rural flocks.

One of only two children, 'as is necessary for salvation', Edwin John Rupert Tobias was born at Lisburn, County Antrim, Northern Ireland, on 26 January 1916, and is therefore a British citizen. But his curate father, originally a Methodist, moved the family to Dublin when Edwin was only four months old. He recollects his childhood:

> When I was a boy in Dublin, just fifteen minutes on the bicycle would take you to the heart of the country. Our family life revolved around the church, of course, and Mother was always a great support to Father in his ministry. We had a very busy social life, and always lived in a big rectory with a parlour maid and cook.
>
> I was always very fond of roast beef, which was very cheap then. I loved sausages, too. And when I was a very little fellow my idea of a good tea was plain bread and butter and cups of tea. But one day I disgraced Mother when she took me out to tea, turning down all these sweet things offered by our host, and saying, 'No thank you, I'll have a good tea when I get home.'

After high school, Edwin took a Bachelor of Arts and then a Master's degree, and also followed a divinity course at Trinity College, Dublin from 1934 to 1940. He never considered any career outside the church, his father being a great influence on him: 'As the old cock crows, the young one learns.'

In 1940 Edwin was made deacon at St Ann's Cathedral, Belfast, for the curacy of Donaghadee, and in 1941 was ordained priest in Christ Church Cathedral, Dublin, for the curacy of Drumcondra and North Strand. 'It was a grand parish, working with such devoted people near the docks. In those days church would always be full on a Sunday evening and you wouldn't get a seat. The singing was wonderful, it nearly lifted the roof off.'

Edwin moved south in 1944 when he was appointed resident preacher in St Fin Barre's Cathedral, Cork, where he remained for five years. In 1945 he married Miriam Hanna (Merrie) on just £300 per year, 'and I was paid only once every three months. But a house was provided for us in Cathedral Close'. The following year, in 1946, Edwin began a long and close association with the Irish countryside when he was appointed rector of Durrus, a hilly parish in west Cork:

They were very poor, but beautiful, wonderful people, many of whom came to church on foot every Sunday morning and to vestry meetings on horseback.

I well remember my first funeral there. These people lived in a little cottage, and on the way we had to pick up the carpenter to take the bedroom window out, as the stairs were too difficult for the coffin. Beforehand the relatives had handed me a paper bag, inside which was a cypress, a white cotton sash about three yards long with a rosette. There was a sash for my hat, too. They liked us to wear that, though hardly any clergy wear hats now. The hearse driver had to wear one, too.

Like other funerals then, it was a tremendous social occasion, and people from all over came for three days before. All were fed, with roast chicken and ham and so on, and the local women helped with the barm bracks [currant loaves]. The drink was there too, including more than a bit of the hard stuff. At every wake there would be chairs around the bed with the people chatting away to each other. Then after a while they'd get up and go and have tea and cakes. It was very hard on most people to produce so much food. And many people only came for the feed and were not known to anyone. Nowadays they're trying to do away with the wakes, and I've always encouraged people to get the body to the church as soon as possible.

Even on such serious occasions Edwin could always see the lighter side of life. So when one of the mourners said: 'Excuse me sir, I'd like to introduce you to the corpse's brother', Edwin was secretly very amused. He continues:

We had some well-off people in the parish, but we always had more fun with the poor.

Later on, when we were in County Meath, there was a man called Movie McCormack, which I thought was very appropriate for an undertaker. And another time someone said to me, 'I can't go to the funeral: will a box of chocolates do instead?' But a lot of people couldn't see the humour. It's not something that can be acquired, and some people I've known have had none whatsoever.

[In those days the Durrus district was very isolated.] One family lived right up on the hill and never saw anybody for weeks on end. A car was essential for my work, and I'd had one since 1945. When the time came to change this old Ford I thought I wouldn't get much for it, as it was all tied up with string. But I managed to sell it to a farmer's wife because she just happened to want a black car. Unfortunately for me, in those days everybody knew the cleric's car and when subsequently it was seen outside all the pubs and bars, they thought I still owned it!

There was a pony and trap to take the children to school, and very few people had cars. But if anyone gave me a lift he would say: 'Would you get in the north door?' For some reason everything was east and west then, and not just road directions.

As a rural rector's wife, Miriam, too, had to be very adaptable. 'One day a woman said to me, "Here's a chicken". I said, "Thank you very much", but when I put my hand inside the bag I found the bird was still alive! Fortunately, our cleaner – a great big capable woman – killed it.'

In 1947 a clergyman 'from the Gold Coast or somewhere' visited Edwin at Durrus. 'He was as black as coal, and when he preached the people came in droves; though it was hard to distinguish between missionary zeal and mere curiosity. He looked splendid in his white robes, though one little girl was worried about the black coming off on the rectory sheets.'

The two maids at the rectory were discussing the visitor while at their scrubbing, and were overheard by Miriam: 'One said: "Is his hair black?" "Yes," the other replied. Then: "Are his hands black?" "Yes," came the answer. But before the inquisitive girl could probe indecently further her companion commented forcefully: "Glory be, *every* part of him is black!"'

After the service, Edwin took the old black canon up to the rectory for a whiskey, 'as he looked so cold. I gave him one and said: "There's water in the jug". To my astonishment, he replied: "Thank you very much, but I wouldn't spoil good Irish whiskey with water".'

'. . . but when I put my hand inside the bag I found the bird was still alive!'

Edwin's predecessor at Durrus had been a great matchmaker. 'Some people there told me they never met their husbands till they got to the church door on the day of the wedding, which was more of a business transaction. Once I was asked to help, but I refused to have anything to do with an alliance, because if anything went wrong I'd be for it. There was always a dowry involved. One man refused, simply because the girl's farmer father could only raise £150 rather than the £200 required. A lot of the old mothers certainly ruined their sons' lives, and many of the husbands were bullied.'

Superstition, too, could prevent or spoil a marriage. Edwin especially remembers one at Durrus where the groom's parents strongly opposed the union because a weasel had been 'dancing' on the kitchen table. 'When someone was being introduced to the bride his reaction was: "I'll never shake hands to a weasel". On another occasion our maid was terribly upset when a robin came into our kitchen. She was sure this meant there would be a death.'

A good way for the rector to get to know the people better was through helping with the harvest:

Farms were so small then; the biggest in Durrus had maybe only three hours thrashing, so we followed the machine all over the district. Sadly, there were some nasty accidents as there was always booze around, and drink and open machinery – especially of the old type – don't mix. But the people were always cute enough not to drink while I was there. At a house we'd have tea, then I'd go out with a pike to help before going back in for more tea.

At Durrus in 1946 the Roman Catholic priest would pass me on the road and not recognise me; however, that sort of thing wouldn't happen now. Indeed, when I left Kilbixy, in 1977, I even had a present from the Catholic community. But thrashing was always an interdenominational effort because at grass roots all the people are great friends. If only the Roman Catholic church would let the Church of Ireland and Church of England people go to the church and take their communion, then there'd be a great change.

If Edwin ever wanted to find out what was going on at Durrus he simply went down to the creamery, 'where everyone brought their milk in between nine and eleven in the morning'. And in the 1940s, with a lot of IRA activity, even a rural rector had to be alert to suspicious circumstances:

One day I was just off to visit somebody when two men got out of a car and went into the grave-yard carrying a spade and a long box. Well, I was responsible for the place, so I thought I'd better make enquiries. But by the time I got over there the box was already in the grave. I said, 'Excuse me, but I'm rector of this parish and I think I should ask you what you're doing.' One of the men, who was a Roman Catholic – we have mixed graveyards – looked up and declared: 'My son's leg is in that box!' I replied: 'That's OK, then', and left them to it.

Another time we found a little dog wrapped in an electric blanket. But there was a name on the blanket, and later we discovered that a chauffeur had been sent sixty miles to bury it! When the Guards [Guarda] went to see the gentle lady who had sent it, she answered the door with a gun!

In 1949 Edwin became rector of Timoleague, Cork; and in 1955 his father – the Archdeacon of Dublin – appointed him curate for the parish of Holy Trinity, Rathmines, Dublin, a very rare example of father and son working together within the clergy. But the countryside called again, and in 1959 Edwin began eighteen years as rector of Kilbixy Union, in the diocese of Meath. His last appointment was in 1977 when he became curate-in-charge of Killucan Union, also in Meath; he retired from the ministry in 1982.

Of all these parishes, Kilbixy was Edwin's favourite, despite the ghosts. 'When we went there, the people asked if we would be living in the haunted rectory. We didn't mind, but were still surprised when we heard knocking on the door and there was no one there. However, we never mentioned this if we had visitors stopping!

'We also had a very lucky escape at Kilbixy, when the church roof collapsed just forty-eight hours after I was taking service. Nobody would have been taken out alive.' Bats, too, bedevilled worshippers at Kilbixy:

At Almorita church Merrie was playing the organ when a bat was seen on the holy table. An old lady came in and said she didn't mind dealing with it. So she covered it with a scarf, took it outside and shook it out. But when she went back in the bat was still there. She must have thought she had lifted it. Eventually a farmer took it out in his hand.

I'm terrified of bats, and we've had to have lots of them removed from rectory attics and water tanks. Once at Timoleague there was one hanging on the dining room curtain. Another time there were two in our bedroom when we went home at Killucan, and once there was one behind the hymn board when we took it down at Kilbixy.

Undaunted by ghosts, bats and the roof falling in, Kilbixy's parishioners were extremely devoted. 'One Sunday Tommy Burnett's car was in dock, and I said: "There won't be many in tonight as Tommy always brings a carful." But later I heard a vehicle on the avenue of the church, and when I looked out, there was Tommy with a tractor and trailer full with people!'

It seems that Kilbixy folk were truly fired up by Edwin's sermons. Indeed, once when he was preaching, lightning was dancing on the wires coming into the church. Afterwards, one of the parishioners said to him: 'That was a very dramatic sermon you gave, lit up in the pulpit, enveloped in fire and brimstone'. But on other occasions lightning was far from welcome, such as when it blew the rectory telephone box off the wall, and in one night killed thirty head of cattle belonging to a local lady farmer.

The boys from a local boarding school only attended church on dry days. 'This was because their building was a bit primitive and they had no facilities for drying coats. So when it rained they used the school chapel. They were certainly very spirited lads, and one day even let an alarm clock off at the back during my service!'

There was plenty of fun with the adult parishioners, too. 'One chap came rushing over to see me at two in the morning, his car headlights blazing up through the rectory window. He had more than a few jars on him, but was so pleased at having just left his mother-in-law in hospital that he had felt compelled to come and tell me! Unfortunately we were looking after a baby then, and he woke that up, too. He said, "I knew I was drunk, but not that drunk!" '

Other nocturnal activities in the Westmeath and Longford area included cockfighting. 'They still do it, most at about one or two o'clock in the morning. Quite a few folk have told me they have woken up and seen a crowd of people in their field. Once we had a lovely cock and one morning we discovered that one of its spurs had been lost overnight.'

It was not really surprising that such ancient sport continued into modern times when some of the participants still lived in relatively primitive conditions. 'Even in my last parish of Killucan, where I was in office from 1977 to 1982, some people still had houses with earthen floors and oil lamps. Some of them had the money to improve things, but simply didn't want to spend it. When one couple on a farm went to retire to a small home they found that all their bank notes, which they had put in a drawer, had been shredded by mice.'

It was as well that Edwin had a great sense of humour to sustain him through his long ministry, because there was always a very sad side to his work as well. As Merrie said, 'There was always a lot of tragedy. Sometimes I was afraid to answer the phone, which would ring mornings and evenings all the year round. Then Edwin would have to go off and tell the relatives.'

With their only son, Christopher, away in Dublin, Merrie and Edwin now live in the delightful Sue Ryder House at Ballyroan, County Laois, with the church and green fields close by. Although he has lived in cities, there is no doubt that Edwin has been more enlightened by the countryside. 'Once we stayed in a London hotel, and couldn't stand the noise of the lorries. We arrived back home in Ireland in the cool of the evening, and when we went to bed it was so still we could hear the sound of the cows chewing the cud. It was a wonderful peace.'

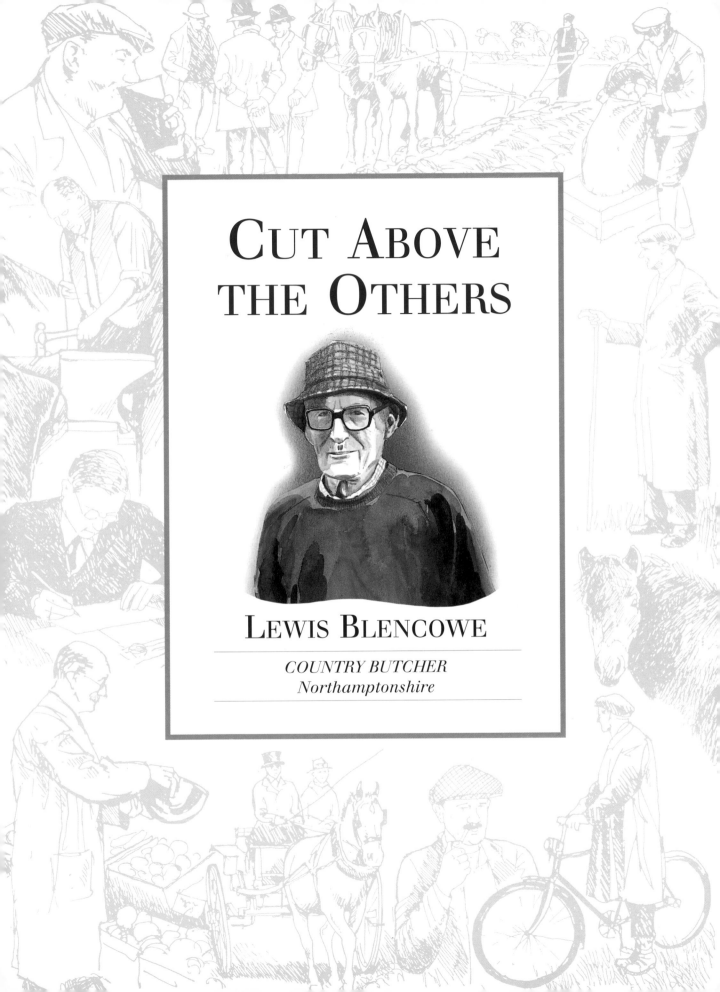

'I don't agree with all this factory farming,' declared retired butcher Lewis Blencowe when we met at his Silverstone home, above and behind the shop which he now lets. 'The pork may *look* better now than it ever did, but where's the taste? No beast is good that's never seen the earth. In the old days every pig was different, with distinctive flavour and colour. And I'd never kill a beast [bullock] until it had two broad teeth, comin' up to two year old, so that it had the right flavour and maturity.

'The other day an old friend said to me: "Wouldn't it be nice if we had consistently good beef every week, like you used to supply?" I always wanted all my customers to have the best of everything. It's nice to think you've pleased people as well as made money.' With such commitment, it's no wonder that Lewis remained a cut above most other butchers throughout a long lifetime in a business which has changed dramatically.

Not content to rest on his laurels and cleaver, during his retirement years Lewis has channelled his endless enthusiasm and energy into growing prize vegetables. The result has been a perennial harvest of cups won at shows throughout the region, and like his meat, his veg have always been as good as they look. And with near-perfect food to fuel him, it's no wonder that Lewis is one of the most youthful octogenarians I have ever encountered.

One of two children, Lewis Mervyn Blencowe was born in the village of Whitfield, near Brackley, on 18 May 1908. In those days this was an area dependent on farming, but it was chiefly his father's success in other fields which inspired Lewis to work so hard and achieve so much. Lewis remembers those days:

Father never stopped. For example, in the April just before I was born there was this terrific deep snow, which Father said took the shape of everything. He told me he had never put up so many spoutings [iron gutterings], as they all came down with the weight of snow.

Grandad went to America to try his hand at farming, but came back within a year. Dad was just a village lad who, with my uncle, was apprenticed as a carpenter and joiner. I can take you now to houses that they built, a tribute to their great craft. Anyway, they did so well they took a bit of land and uncle had the mill farm, where I spent all my time. I had a marvellous childhood there and soon became very fond of horses.

We always used to hear the nightingales, any time. And after the dawn chorus you always heard old Tom Chambers, the wagoner who lived opposite, open the field gate and call the horses, at around 5.30am in the summer. There were fifteen of 'em shod, and they'd come clip-clopping into this stone causeway, along the street and into the horse yard and stable. They were all loose, and some were a bit bossy so Tom would shout at them. Altogether it was a lovely sound in the quiet of the early morning, the shoes on the stones and just this one voice in total command of all that power.

We had fifty working farm horses in Whitfield then, as well as all the driving horses and float horses and so on. Even the builders' carts were pulled by horses. Now on the land you just get in one of those massive machines and press the button. No generation has seen changes like mine. In our village there used to be two men who could never read nor write.

It was wonderful as a boy to take a horse up to Jimmy Baldwin the blacksmith and get it shod, with one man holding the red-hot iron and one striking it. One day there, John Thomas, who had one of the first two cars in the village, didn't put his handbrake on properly so his vehicle ran down the hill and smashed some railings. Amazingly the car wasn't damaged, but John had to pay the smith to repair the railings.

I always looked forward to school holidays as I enjoyed the farm work so much. The Forest binder was pulled by three horses, two on the pole and a third in the front ridden by me or another boy. Harvest used to be so lovely and seemed to go on so long then. Now, unless you actually work on a farm, you hardly know when harvest has started and when it is over.

The earliest thing I can remember was when I was going along with a wagonload of sheaves, and one fell off onto the mare's back and she bolted. The men called out to me: 'Let her go, boy!', and after a good run, during which the wagon had hit the gate-post, she calmed down. I got a good ticking-off.

Another time, when I was fourteen, I had a strong cob which I decided was ready for harness. So I put him in an old trap and went to Brackley, where I was so proud, parading up and down. But just as I was going over the railway bridge a train let off steam and the cob bolted. He ran for 2½ miles, but luckily the only thing we met on the way was a man on a bike who jumped off and hopped over a gate to save himself. Eventually I managed to pull the cob in at Whitfield, after which we went off for a few miles more and he was perfectly all right.

Lewis attended Whitfield school to the age of twelve, after which he went to Brackley Church of England school; he made an excellent drawing of the school, which he still has. He remembers:

Father always wanted to push me on to be an architect, as he built houses an' everything. The family firm made almost everythin' in that workshop – windows, stairs, the lot. The men even did the brickwork and plastering. Father also built wheels and wagons, and did some undertaking besides.

We were lucky to have a very nice house, which Dad built himself on the site of two old thatched cottages, which he knocked down. We were one of the first in the area to have an indoor tap, the water running by gravity after a windmill pumped it up to a reservoir on the hill.

Mum was able to keep working as a schoolteacher as we had a wonderful gran and grandad. He was a chief horseman and at first wouldn't let me have a saddle, so that my feet wouldn't get caught up in the stirrups if I came off.

Even as a schoolboy Lewis was exceptionally independent and had very green fingers:

In that very dry year of 1921 Father bought this small field, and it became my little 'farm' where I reared poultry and goats. Dad was secretary of the allotment association, too, and I was allowed a chain square of my own. I used to go down after school and at weekends to shut in the hens, do the sowing and weeding and suchlike, as well as a bit of work on the farm. The ol' chaps could see I was really keen and used to come along and say: ' 'ere you are boy, 'ere's a few

'The men called out to me: "Let her go, boy!"'

seed potatoes'. One year I put a ton of potatoes in a clamp and one ol' boy used to take a hundredweight a week off me. He was always saying 'Well done boy, they're really nice!' But later on, when I was courtin', those old boys were worried I was 'goin' the wrong way', as my allotment grew the best crop of wild poppies you've ever seen!

Helping hands were always needed at his uncle's water mill, which Lewis often used to operate with his cousin:

Flour hadn't been ground there since Dad was a boy, but we used to grind grist for cattle feed all winter. We booked the farmers in and they brought the grain on floats. Farmers never bought much of anythin' in those days. They really lived off the land.

Us boys had great fun working at the mill. We used to grab the chain, pull a cord and go up through the trap with leather hinges where the sacks used to go. It was a risky business with so much machinery about, and we were often told off. We had a big ol' grease tin and spatula to keep the wooden cogs turning nice.

In April, after the end of grinding corn, we cleared the mill and tidied up ready for sheep washing. In early May we used to do up to about two thousand, all booked in. And we could deal with three flocks at once – one coming down the lane, one holding in Miller's Close (a field), and one in the wash. This was about six feet deep, created by damming the brook, and each sheep was put under a strong spout. In those days lots of sheep fed on the ploughland and got very dirty, so they had to be washed just before shearing to get a better price for the wool; there was great shame on the farmer who didn't bother. Most of them were very generous and would send us boys up the pub to fetch beer in a can while their sheep were being washed. Our millstream was a tributary of the Ouse, and there were other mills working at Turweston and Brackley, all within a few miles.

But there was at least one day when the sheep in Lewis' care were far from co-operative:

On a Saturday when I was about fourteen I was taking about 150 wild Cheviots on the road with my cousin. We had a good sheepdog, but it was a very humid day and this made the sheep restless.

As we passed a row of alms-houses on a bend a couple of sheep shot through a pale-gate which wasn't fastened properly, and it closed behind them. Our ol' dog knew they were missin' all right but didn't know where they'd gone. It turned out that the front door of the house was open too, and the sheep had charged right in where this ol' gal, who had no taps or sink, had a big bucket of water on the table – the sheep had upset everything. Well, this ol' dear was standin' there shakin' and I wanted to console her, but I had all those sheep there in the road and couldn't stop.

When we got back to the farm we were very thirsty and given all this rough ol' cider, so by the time we went out to get on our bikes everythin' was goin' round and round. After a bit our front wheels touched and I went one way, my cousin the other, and I just lay there on the bank for a while, very hot and confused. Then there was a terrific thunderstorm and we took shelter at Brackley station.

Other times it was nothing to be sent out with a big drove of bullocks. But you always had to send someone ahead to close all the gates. It wasn't so much them gettin' in the gardens, it was gettin' them out again that was the problem!'

As a boy Lewis never had much time for sport. 'I was always workin'; but we did take a wire occasionally and noose the odd eel along the mill sluice.'

Typical of the time, the village was a close-knit community, where everyone knew and trusted each other. As Lewis describes:

No one locked up then. The butcher and baker would let themselves in, and if anyone did lock a door you generally knew where to find the key.

Aunt kept a wonderful little grocer's shop, and our farm supplied milk to the village at 9am and 5pm. She had this stand with a snow-white table-cloth on for the pails of milk, and there was another table next to it where the people left their pans and cans. Aunt always knew whose they all were.

Everybody had good food, all home-grown. Most people killed a bacon pig, and you cooked with suet then to get the flavour. The butcher always came midweek and Saturday with his big horse van and opened up the side. Eight shillings would buy plenty for a week for a whole family.

Local bread was baked almost every day. Dad always said you couldn't beat Gramp [Harry] Humphrey's cottage loaves, which he brought round on a cart pulled by his horse Ginger. To heat his bread oven he used thorn-shank faggots tied up by the hedge-layers. After the faggots were burnt inside the brick oven the ashes were raked out, and Gramp would look at the glow of this pebble set in the back – a kind of early thermostat – to see if the temperature was right for the bread to go in.

There were two bakehouses, one for each end of the village. As well as for bread, they were used for cooking people's dinners. At the weekend, families used to set in at eleven o'clock, then draw their Yorkshire puddings at half past twelve.

There was none of this convenience stuff. The only ice-cream you had was at a fête, though much later on the Walls man used to pedal out into the hayfield with his 'Stop me and buy one'.

When Lewis was a teenager there was still no telephone in Whitfield, so there could be considerable delay in summoning help after an accident. 'When I was fourteen, word came that Andrew Ayres – one of the workers who set the fires in the baker's oven – had chopped his thumb clean off. This lady went to assist and did the best she could, but there was no car, and the fastest transport was my uncle's trap. I can still picture them racing past with Andrew Ayres holding his bandaged hand up in the air, on their way to Brackley cottage hospital.'

On another day it was a very distinguished visitor in need of a telephone at Whitfield. Lewis describes the occasion:

I saw this chap comin' up through the village on horseback late on a winter's afternoon. He was all in red and had been huntin' with the Grafton. He stopped and said: 'Hello. Is there a telephone here?' I said: 'It's the Prince of Wales, isn't it?' and he said, 'Yes.' It was the future King Edward VIII.

'I can still picture them Andrew Ayres holding his hand up in the air…'

I knew the first phone in the area had come into a nearby farm, so I pointed him in the right direction. He went up there and tapped on the door, and poor Elsie the maid was so surprised. The prince gave her half-a-crown, and when I last saw her she still had that actual coin.

An ol' farmer, Freddie Smith, over at Slapton also saw Prince Edward out hunting. Freddie was a real character, with a smock and a bag tied with string round his waist, and he'd always say what he wanted. So when this other ol' chap told him 'That's the Prince of Wales, over there', Freddie scratched his head in his usual way and just called out: 'Ay up. How are you?' But the prince was very good, and came over to shake hands.

I remember very well, too, the girl Alice who came to work at our farm just after the first war. We were all down in the fields busy with the harvest and I was sent back to fetch some tools or something. At the time there was this sow and litter of pigs – all sandy and black, with no white – and as I passed the barn where Alice always hung her dinner, this ol' sow came trotting out holding a pudding basin in her mouth by the cloth wrapped around it. As she ran off I hit her with these sheaves until she dropped the basin. It seemed all right, so I put it back on the hook and said nothing. Later on, when we all sat together at dinner, Alice asked us boys what we were tittering about; but she never knew the truth!

At the age of eighteen Lewis stopped working for his family and became apprenticed to Peredge-Salmon:

This was the leading butcher in Brackley. I was bound over until I was twenty-one, and got £1 a week, 15s of which went to Mother.

In those days all the animals came into town live and we did all our own killing. Imagine bringing cows and pigs into the centre of Brackley now, with all that traffic.

For deliveries we had this wonderful Welsh cob and a London butcher's car, all covered in – not even a fly could enter. We also had shop bikes with carriers and I used to go all over the place to surrounding villages. One of these was Turweston, which was a place of gentry then. There were five or six big houses there, and in the winter there would be over fifty hunters in the village, following the Grafton hounds.

Sometimes I went to Turweston and back six times in a day, but some of those ol' cooks would always have a cup of tea and a big cake for you. The big houses were often let for the hunting season, and then almost every butcher in the district would be on the doorstep fighting for the trade. One day I saw this furniture van going in, so I thought I'd beat the competition, stop off and get a big order. But I had to wait some time to see the housekeeper, and when I got back the boss's wife told me off for being late. But you just had to get the trade then, and my boss knew that, so that Saturday night, when I got my wages, he said 'Well done, boy' and gave me an extra half-a-crown for looking after the business.

When Lewis started courting his future wife, Bella (Frances Isabel), a Yorkshire farmer's daughter, his parents were very wary as she was from 'far away. "How do you know who she is?", they asked. I said: "I know exactly who she is, and what's more I know who she's going to be!" After that they said nothing else!' Lewis recollects those times clearly:

There was one night when I was comin' back from courting that I'll always remember. I was goin' along on my 3½ horsepower BSA motorbike that I'd bought for £12, when I saw this

'. . . this ol' sow came trotting out holding a pudding basin'

bright light comin' and goin' through the trees. So I followed round to it, and there was Cottesford manor house on fire.

The three maids were in night attire and trapped on top by the parapet, and the ol' gent of the house was runnin' about in his dressing-gown with a few books under his arm. There were only one or two other people there and we got a long ladder to fetch the girls down.

After a while the Bicester fire brigade came and they had their first motorised engine, which they couldn't handle. And then came the old Amos horse-drawn vehicle from Brackley. By this time it was towed by a lorry, but I can still remember the two old greys, pensioners from World War I – one with an ear shot off – which used to pull it. These horses were also used by the people who owned the pub for carting stones and other jobs, but if they heard the fire alarm bell they'd go mad and tip up their load because they wanted to get moving. They knew where they'd got to go all right!

Lewis in July 1928, aged twenty

Anyway, this night I knew all the Brackley chaps, who wondered what on earth I was doing there, and they damned soon pumped the pond dry, while the Bicester crew, struggling with their new vehicle, got nowhere. But it was all in vain, and nothing could be salvaged. I looked through the French windows, and there was this lovely grand piano which suddenly came alive with flame; then it went bang and collapsed, and all the keys went everywhere. The owners had an old bloodhound, too, but he was never seen again. When we left at 3am the house was just a shell, with the water-tanks hanging in the roof. It took me ages to find my motorbike then, too, because I'd just thrown it down behind a wall in a rush and couldn't remember where.

On completing his apprenticeship, Lewis started work straight away:

I went to a top man in Brackley. But when he retired he didn't let me have the business as he'd promised. So I got very itchy feet, as I wanted to work on my own, especially as I'd already married in 1931, when we'd bought a little cottage for £150; besides which, wages were only £2 10s for a top man working seventy or eighty hours a week.

So I looked at this ol' broken-down business, Jarvis's, just up the road at Syresham, and got it reserved till the Tuesday. I asked Father what he thought, and he took me into Barclays to see the manager, in about 1934. I needed £100 just to go into the rented premises, and then we hadn't even finished paying for our house. The shop had no fridge, only a deep cellar, and a lot of the tackle was useless. But the price did include an ol' Morris van and we was always pre-

CUT ABOVE THE OTHERS

pared to have a go. Anyway, the bank man let me have £200 to get started, and he said: 'Don't be mean, but look after the ha'pennies!'

Among the first things I did was pay a friend to put in electricity, and get a fridge. Uncle had left the rented mill farm, so we let our house to him at 5s 6d a week, and he lived there till a great age.

One of the reasons why Lewis got off to a good start at Syresham was that he had 'a few good ol' pals' to help him. In his own words:

One of them said: 'Should you want some pigs any time you can 'ave 'em off me at only so much a score dead weight'.

The first time I took ol' man Payne up on this I scrubbed out the delivery van and put in some straw to collect the animals. You can imagine what the hygiene people would think about that now. Anyway, when I went to get the first few pigs he helped me load and then went over to open the gate; he obviously didn't want his sons to hear him speak to me as I drove through. He said: 'Boy, if you've got anyone else to pay before me, don't you worry, I knows what it's like setting up in business.' Ain't that a wonderful thing for him to say. You'd be lucky to get help like that nowadays.

Things went well, and Lewis soon built up a marvellous business:

Each week I killed two bullocks, ten lambs and about four pigs. I never minded the slaughtering side of it and was always as kind as possible to the animals. It's a job you haven't to push yourself at – if a chap worked up a sweat you knew he'd be no good at it. When I first started I just pole-axed the bullocks. For the pigs I had a wonderful mallet which I made myself, and they'd roll over beautiful before I slit 'em. But it was a skilful job and you'd have to be accurate with the knife as it was only narrow where the main artery was, next to the food passage.

Humane killers came in just before the war, but the 'bell' one was dangerous to the operator as you had these hard blue bricks and the bullet could ricochet anywhere. In any case, slaughtering was always very hard work, with pulley blocks and so on, but I've done hundreds by myself. Fortunately in all my years butchering and farming I've never broken a bone, even though I've been lain on, kicked and thrown many a time.

In 1938 everythin' was comin' wonderful. It was the best period I ever had, with good, steady family business. In the thirties rump and fillet was only about 1s 4d a pound, brisket 8d and stewing steak 10d to 1s. For most people chicken and turkey was only ever a treat at Christmas, but you got proper birds then, which were kept longer and fed better.

But the good times were soon to change with the outbreak of war. Lewis sold his old business and bought half of the old Manor Farm at Syresham, a hundred acres; but as hostilities continued, he was increasingly bogged down by bureaucracy:

It would have been a lot easier if I'd gone to war. With rationing we were formed into butchers' groups, seventeen of us in Brackley and Rural District, and we were allocated meat according to permit through the only stock buyer – the Ministry of Food. I got roped in more and more, and was made secretary of the group, which involved a lot of extra work, such as going to Brackley at 5am several days a week to allocate meat. It was a hell of a job as the butchers' permits varied every week. And you had to report in all weathers. With no antifreeze, sometimes you had to boil a kettle to get the vehicle goin', and very often go out with Jerry flyin' over the top.

I was also a cattle grader, and for all this I only ever got expenses. At first we used to assess many animals by hand as there was no weighing for sheep, but cattle could be weighed at the gasworks. But us practical chaps were happy to weigh by hand; it wasn't much trouble. I could work day and night then and never got tired. I reckoned I could do it sleep walkin'.

One of Lewis' most vivid wartime memories is of the time when Coventry was bombed:

You could hear these ol' planes droning over with their heavy loads on, then *bmmm-bmmm-bmmm* as they dropped their bombs, followed by the singing noise of the lightened aircraft veering away. We had some terrible dos then when the planes thought they was somewhere else. One night they killed all these cattle and I had to go out to put the wounded ones out of their misery.

After the war, things got even worse for butchers. Quite apart from the bitter winter of 1946–7, when it was so bad getting about you had to buy slatted headlamp covers for your vehicle to throw the light down on the snow, rationing was kept on far too long. But I was determined to rebuild everything. They'd already confiscated our best field with a compulsory purchase for housing, so I sold up all the land and buildings at Syresham in 1948, and in the year of the first Grand Prix, came here to Silverstone where I bought this shop and ten acres down the road.

With that 8d meat ration, it was the worst ol' driest time you ever 'ad; but when rationing ended, I was prepared. I got the ol' slaughterhouse ready out the back here, and declared I was going back to how I'd left off in 1938. By then the wholesalers had come in, but I said 'No, I'm not havin' meat brought here by nobody. I'll kill my own, as we used to.' And that's what I did with another butcher nearby. We'd slaughter three beasts [cattle] a week, one for him and two for me. I had my ring of farmers, and I knew exactly where the cattle could be fed and where they couldn't.

'. . . rationing was kept on far too long.'

SYRESHAM

NORTHANTS

OSBORNE & SON, F.A.I.

Are favoured with instuctions from Mr. L. M. Blencowe (having sold the farm) to Sell by Auction on the premises known as "BELL LANE" on

MONDAY, 27th SEPTEMBER, 1948

at 2 p.m. prompt

The whole of the

Live & Dead Farming Stock

comprising

17 Head of CATTLE

7 D.C. Cows & Heifers; 2 Barreners; 7 Heifer Calves (6-8 months) LINCOLN RED Pedigree Bull (3 yrs.) Good Stock getter & bred by Messrs Reid & Sigrist, Leicester.

2 HORSES

br. gelding (9 yrs.) Good worker all gears; Rn. Cob (aged) (Well known in the district).

12 Head of POULTRY

Sussex Cks. (Messrs. Turney strain)

together with

IMPLEMENTS & MACHINERY

FORDSON TRACTOR rubbers on rear (excellent condition); 2-furr. Ransome Plough; Cambride Tractor Roll; Flat roll (1 h) Massey Harris Disc. drill (for tractor); 1 h. Hay Sweep; Set Adkinhead Harrows; Seed & drag Harrows; Massey Harris Binder; Albion Mower for Tractor (equal to new); Hay Loader; Horse Rake; Blackstone Swath Turner; Ladders (34 & 20 rds); 4-wh. Trolley (for horse or tractor) with side boards; Hay holders; Rick Sheet 24 ft. × 18 ft.; Wagon Sheet; Farm tip Cart on rubbers (with raves); 4 h.p. Lister Engine on Trolley; Root Pulper (unchokeable); Milk Float; 120 Gal. Paraffin Tank; Sheep troughs, Hay Knives; etc. etc.

HARNESS. Set thiller; Set Cob; G.O. Tackle etc. etc.

DAIRY UTENSILS : Cooler & hopper; Buckets, strainer. etc.

No Catalogues.   On view morning of Sale

Further particulars apply : The Auctioneers; Land Agency Offices, Buckingham (phone 2120).

Farm auction details from when Lewis sold up in 1948

Eventually Lewis was helped by Silverstone's development and growing fame as a top motor-racing venue, although he was increasingly called out to destroy animals injured in road accidents. But during his first years there it was more traditional work which made his business thrive. 'Much of the land around here is not good for cultivation, but it is good for forestry, so Silverstone was a big timber village with a great many big-eating people wanting good food. Everything had to be quality. However, it wasn't the increasing number of visitors I relied on, but providing a reliable product for local families. If you hadn't wanted meat one week I'd want to know why. At first the disruption caused by the building of the race-track, and then on race days themselves was terrible, but we did get to supply some contractors. Now my shop tenant welcomes visitors.'

Consistent quality was vital. 'If you made a real country sausage the secret was always keepin' 'em right. You don't alter 'em if they sell well because people will only ever have one bad sausage and they won't have any more. It's what people say about you that counts.' But there was also a right approach in handling customers. In Lewis' opinion:

To serve, you haven't got to be a wooden man, but you must adapt. If our most gracious queen came in I could serve her just as I could deal with an ol' diehard from the village. People must have faith in you. But you can also tempt them. I'd cut a steak in front of them in such a way that it fell down right, and they couldn't resist a second one.

Today a lot of butchers wouldn't know how to cut things like a proper saddle of lamb and a wing rib of beef. They couldn't cure a ham or prepare an ox tongue. I used to sell two pickled tongues a week. For that you must be very clean and accurate with your mix of salts, else they won't last. I could never get enough of 'em, but few are sold now. People are more interested in all this barbecue business, which never used to come into it.

We sold a few pheasants and hares, but never used to push 'em as it was mainly a good, traditional family business. Rabbits were never a big seller as so many people caught their own, and they mostly went out with myxomatosis. There wasn't much call for geese, either. People always wanted good farm turkeys and chickens at Christmas, and I daren't face the festive season without forty pickled ox tongues, so then I had to buy a few from a wholesaler.

Another thing today is that meat's handled too much. If you haven't got to touch it, then don't. Always stick a hook in it and hang it up. Also there's all these stupid rules now, with Europe insisting on things like a plastic block. It's a wonder they don't want plastic knives. But there's been no improvement in hygiene. In the old days a butcher's pride and joy was his block and his benches all scrubbed clean. You were judged on that. You can give one chap everythin' there is for modern cleanliness, and another one a good old-fashioned place, and it won't make any difference – if a chap's goin' to wipe his nose on the back of his hand, he'll do so when you're not there. You can't be too clean. No, your food today is definitely handled too much, and the individual craftsman has died out.

With the ending of rationing, Lewis was in great demand as a stock judge all over the country. Unfortunately most of the main shows came just before Christmas, when Lewis was already very busy with special orders. But with his great experience in butchery and farming he was the ideal man to judge an animal's conformation. They used to call him 'the bloke that looked through 'em'. 'But as well as looking, it's in these!', said Lewis, holding his hands up. 'People used to rely on my fingers.'

One fatstock show at Winslow provided a good illustration of why Lewis was also known as 'the man with X-ray eyes'. Lewis relates this occasion:

My fellow judge was a British beef buyer and I thought, 'I've got a bright spark here!' As soon as we started I could tell he was hopeless, always letting me decide and then agreeing all the time.

Eventually all the prizewinners were called out to decide the championships. I was working on this beast and putting it down to reserve champion when all of a sudden, for the first time, this chap didn't agree. So I pressed him and told him to handle the pair, which he did, and then he agreed with me. After that he was a bit niggly for the rest of the day. He'd obviously let himself be influenced by the crowd.

As it turned out, the same butcher bought both champion and reserve, so I was happy about that. And both owners were at the abbatoir to see how their beasts came out. When they saw the carcasses they immediately shook hands in agreement that the best animal had won, confirming that I had been right all along.

*Lewis was in great demand
as a stock judge*

Lewis, too, would sometimes buy a champion animal, 'so that you got into the local paper, and this boosted your business. And it's nice for the public to see that the judge has the strength of his own convictions. I would pay up to about £600 for a beast over twenty years ago, so sometimes your pal would say you were a fool. I still buy a few beasts for my tenant. The odd thing is that they're now auctioned by the kilo, but still sold in the shop by the pound. Luckily I have no trouble converting!'

Good horses, too, were irresistible to Lewis:

Country butchers always used to have a good cob, and I've done a lot of driving; for years I had the fastest cob around here. There used to be some challenges between us, but nine times out of ten someone would call it off if they saw you go beforehand. In the old days I could never see any danger, but then you don't when you're younger. Eventually, as I was going off to a show, my wife said: 'Don't you bring another horse back today'.

One day a friend said to me: 'How can you stand all that hard work slaughtering?' So for the last few years I was persuaded to use a good abbatoir run by friends at Northampton. I retired from butchery at the age of sixty-four.

Since then Lewis has remained exceptionally active. Even in his late eighties he has continued his lifelong interest in hunting, often following the Stowe School Beagles for six or seven miles on foot. He describes his sport:

I've been a member since it was formed, and I shall go with my terrier as long as I can. I also follow the Grafton and have ridden with them on the odd occasion. I've always loved it, since we first sang John Peel.

The Stowe is one of the best beagle packs in the country. Us older boys can't keep up quite like we used to, so we find a good vantage point and just watch. Some places are still OK for hares, but it's very variable from day to day. I always say to people, 'You can come if you pay the cap, but don't expect anythin' marvellous: it doesn't always happen!' Also, it's all becoming more difficult for hunting as there's always another road comin' through and cuttin' the country up. With most of the big estates split up there's a lot more landowners, and if just one refuses us permission to cross his land it can cut off a big area of countryside.

Like everyone else, we've had our share of trouble with the anti-fieldsports brigade, such as in 1993, when we met at Lower Boddington. The antis had been to upset the Bicester and met us along the way, and we couldn't get the hounds out the trailer. But overall it's not so bad now, as they're being made to toe the line more. I've never been attacked, but I've been abused a lot. They generally breathe somethin' awful as they go past, such as 'You ought to have been dead long ago', and if you answer 'em they start on. Unfortunately for me I'm apt to get in the middle of it, so when one girl went to take my photograph I very soon told her what I'd do. I don't see why anyone else should interfere with our great traditions.

Throughout the spring and summer Lewis spends most of his time in his half-acre garden nurturing huge vegetables such as leeks, onions and celery. Every year he spends hundreds of hours, sometimes working till late at night, lovingly preparing the best and biggest of his produce for some eight to ten shows within about a twenty-five-mile radius. It's not surprising that some of the cups for individual vegetables and collections have returned to his trophy cupboard year after year.

With such strong interests to keep him at home, Lewis has 'never been a holiday man. I've always enjoyed the calendar of the year, from sowing and showing to harvest and hunting. And I've never been to a Grand Prix, even though the circuit is on my doorstep. Nowadays there's enough of a race-track outside my front door, and you have to say a prayer before crossing the road. But if I got knocked down tomorrow I couldn't complain because I've had a grand life. A man's greatest blessing is to have a good wife and partner by his side, as I did for 55½ years, and a good family. Now I'm well looked after with all three daughters still living in the parish, and I have four grandsons and three great grandchildren.'

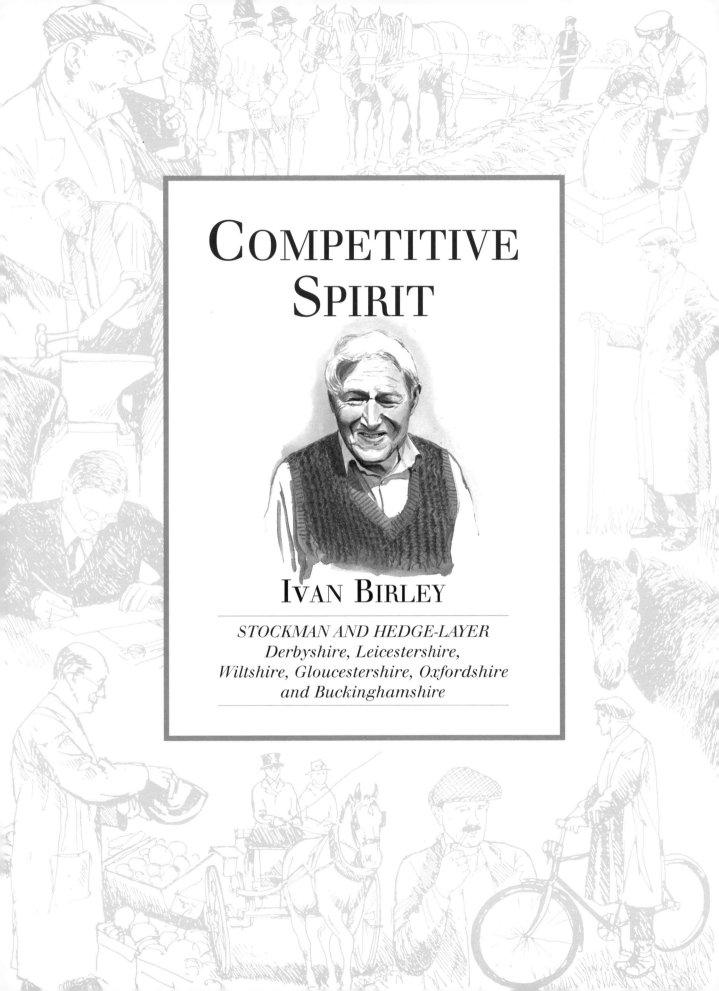

COMPETITIVE SPIRIT

IVAN BIRLEY

STOCKMAN AND HEDGE-LAYER
Derbyshire, Leicestershire,
Wiltshire, Gloucestershire, Oxfordshire
and Buckinghamshire

In 1993, 88-year-old Ivan Birley was given a conservation award by the BBC's *Country File* television programme. But it was by no means the first trophy on his bulging Buckinghamshire sideboard. Throughout his long life Ivan has striven to be top of the tree, both at work and play: not only has he shown others the way with prize-winning hedges and cattle, but he has also won many trophies for darts and dominoes. But then, he did gain great inspiration from his father, a competitor of equal renown.

Proudly, Ivan told me that his father 'was the first man in England to breed tri-coloured mice: Highfield Sensation, Highfield Fredricka and Highfield Josephia, which were black, white and tan'. To mark the 1905 achievement, the splendidly named National Mouse Club awarded Birley senior a beautiful silver medal, which Ivan still treasures.

Rather appropriately, Ivan was also a product of that prize-winning year, being born on 28 November at Long Eaton, in Derbyshire. One of eleven children, of whom he is the sole survivor, he was the son of a lacemaker by trade, but a countryman by instinct. 'Dad was always showing vegetables, and in 1913 he had a bronze medal for kidney beans at Crystal Palace. He also used to judge rabbits, and the cottage I was born in was named 'Ancona' after the fowls he used to show.

'In 1913 we went to live at Risley, where Dad took two acres of ploughland and six acres of grass, though he still worked at the factory. He took orders for vegetables, and me and me brother would deliver them with a barrow in the evenings. Also, when I was just eight we went muck-knocking – scattering the cows' heaps about the fields with a fork – for sixpence a day on a nearby farm.'

When he was 12½, Ivan began his long association with cattle, milking half-a-dozen

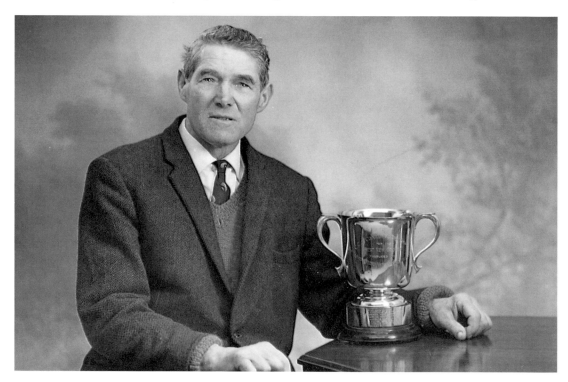

Ivan with the Coape-Arnold trophy which he won for the best year's growth in 1966, in competition with 160 hedge-layers

70

cows at 6am and again after school, on a farm at Long Eaton. At the age of thirteen he was taken on full-time. 'You could leave school then if you had put in so many attendances. I also had to pulp mangolds in a machine and put hay through a chaffcutter for cattle feed, and help put the bedding straw in the barn when the thrasher came round.'

In 1918 Ivan left home for the first time, to live and work on a farm at Chaddesden. 'I worked for a dealer who used to go off and buy about four hundred sheep and cattle at a time. Every Tuesday and Friday I walked the three miles with the drover into Derby market, and I'd already done another three fetchin' 'em up from by the river. But the drover walked much further than me. He came all the way from Ilkeston and would gather up various lots

---

FARMERS WEEKLY

NATIONAL HEDGE-LAYING & DITCHING CONTEST
The Fields, Lowfield Heath, Surrey, 3rd March, 1966.

This is to certify that

IVAN P. BIRLEY

WON COAPE – ARNOLD CHALLENGE TROPHY. PRIZE

IN THE BEST YEARS GROWTH CLASS

DATED THIS DAY 2nd MARCH 1967

Editor

---

of cattle along the way. My pay was ten bob a week, and no "nine-to-five" days.'

Then Ivan moved to a farm at Repton, where he had to feed and muck out the cattle, all shorthorns. He describes the routine:

> In winter they was tied up in sheds in individual stalls and let out into the yard to get water twice a day. In summer they were out in the fields and tied up twice a day for milking. In those days there was no proper record of milk yields on most farms, and as long as a bull looked like a bull, that was all right. A shorthorn heifer used to give about one gallon a day and a cow about three gallons, but today it's all scientific and the yields have increased steadily since the war. Now in decent herds a heifer can give five gallons and a cow six or seven gallons.
>
> After the first war, things were very different. Long Eaton became a ghost town. You used to be able to hear all the clatter-bang of the lace-making machines, but they were all closed down.

In 1923, at seventeen years of age, Ivan joined the army and went to Egypt and India with the Leicesters. His time was up in 1931 'when Ghandi was on the go', but he had to stay on for an extra six months 'for the trooping season: in those days troop ships only came to India from September to March'.

Ivan married in 1931, when he was on a vocational training course to be a chauffeur/gardener at Swindon; but then he was unemployed for eighteen months. Eventually he moved back to Long Eaton and worked for a company making artificial silk at Spondon.

Just before World War II he went to work on a farm near Swindon. As he was in a reserved occupation he pretended to be a 'bombed-out shopkeeper' when applying to join the army, but he was still turned down. So he remained in farming for the rest of his working life,

mostly in the Midlands and Cotswolds, and the last thirty years on a farm at Oakley, in Buckinghamshire.

It was during the war that Ivan started hedge-laying. 'I was working on a farm near Great Dalby, in Leicestershire, when this old chap of seventy-one showed me how to go on. As a cattle-man it was quite a natural thing to learn because a good stockman is a good fencer and hedger; he doesn't want to see his stock get out, so he makes his fences sound.'

Hedge-laying has always been most widely practised in areas where stock farming has predominated. Although it is an ancient craft, it was undertaken on a relatively small scale until many thousands of miles of hedges were planted with the Enclosure Acts and Awards of the eighteenth and nineteenth centuries. Throughout most of the second half

Ivan's hedge-laying has been an example to many

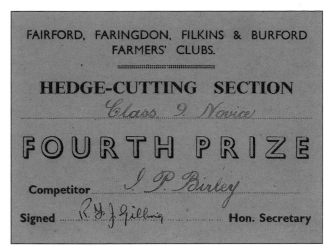

FAIRFORD, FARINGDON, FILKINS & BURFORD
FARMERS' CLUBS.

HEDGE-CUTTING SECTION

Class 9 Novice

F O U R T H   P R I Z E

I P Birley

Competitor

Signed *R Y J Gilling* .... Hon. Secretary

of the twentieth century the craft has rapidly declined, as hedgerows have been ripped out to make way for larger fields and more crops. At the same time mechanisation has greatly reduced manpower so that the remaining farm workers are generally far too busy to do any hedge-laying. However, there is now renewed interest in this fascinating craft, as its benefits to conservation and landscape are increasingly recognised.

In the old days, hedging was always a winter activity because most other farm work was slack then and it kept the labourers busy as well as the hedges manageable and tidy. Also, with most of the herbage down, it was obviously easier to see and get at the job. Over the years Ivan has done most of his hedging between September and May, but he has worked in every month of the year. Let him describe his craft in his own words:

With the leaves on it's only tricky at first, and there is the advantage that it's better for cutting with the sap up. You must be specially careful in late winter, as then the wood is brittle and comes off easily.

The first thing to learn is how to sharpen your tools properly. The main tool is the billhook – God knows how many different styles there are. This is my best one; it cost me £3 10s over thirty years ago. It's not quite a Derbyshire one and not quite a Leicestershire one.

Then there's your axe – I've always had a 4lb and a 7lb one; and a long-handled slasher: there's several different shapes of these. I've had my 7lb stake hammer since 1932. Your mittens are always thick leather because the thorn is so sharp, but in my early seventies I started using a chainsaw and you need fingers for that. Unfortunately the modern gloves don't last like the old mittens. But one good new thing is the shredder. Before that we had to burn all the rubbish.

I lost my hedge tools once, back in the bitter winter of 1962–3. After working on Christmas Eve I put my things under some brushwood, and then the big blizzards came and covered it all up so I didn't know where the tools were. I couldn't get them back till the March thaw. We had to dig ourselves out the house several times, and the indoor tank froze so we had to get water from a cattle trough that was surrounded by straw. The snow got so hard the sheep could walk on top.

There are several different styles of hedge-laying. The Midland style, which *Farmer's Weekly* [the long-standing farmers' magazine] called the Bullock, originates from Leicestershire and has got to be a big, strong hedge to stop a bullock. Then the Welsh have their own style of hedge altogether, only three feet high on account of the stock being all sheep. The Lancashire and Westmorland style has stakes both sides, and the Derbyshire is similar to ours but there are no binders [heathers] on top to keep it all tight. With the South of England style, brush is put both sides to stop sheep and cattle nibbling new shoots. But with ploughland hedging you don't need brush as there's no stock around. Nevertheless it still reduces wind damage to crops.

When the blizzards came, Ivan lost all his hedge tools

Some hedges are centuries old, and regular laying prevents them getting too spindly. Ivan has tackled one not cut for forty years, but ideally a hedge needs laying every fifteen to twenty years; and Ivan has been at it long enough to do some hedges twice. 'After laying you let the hedge grow for about five years, then trim it for about five years, then leave it for about five years before laying again.'

Ivan admits that hedging can be a lonely job, which is why he takes his old dog Jane along 'for a bit of company. And before her, my border collie, Jim.' He describes the attraction of the work, and the technique required:

The job is never monotonous. Every hedge is different. It's like a jigsaw puzzle, and you've got to get into the bones of it before you can solve it. You use your billhook, or axe, on thicker wood, to cut about three-quarters way through the branch you want to bend over, but you must leave enough wood to let the sap come up. You place your stakes – hazel or other wood, brought with you or cut from the hedge – every eighteen inches apart, and weave the pleaches [cut stems] at the same angle around them. As the work progresses, you hammer the stakes home and they are left to rot away or be removed when the hedge is established.

In competition it is essential to have the stakes at equal distance and in a straight line. If heathers [cut hazel or elm rods] are woven between the stake tops to make the job neat, and to help keep the naturally springy thorn in place, they must be joined together properly. When I'm judging I always give a good shake to test for strength, and I don't like to see stakes left too high. And if the job's done properly there will be plenty of tillering [new shoots] in the hedge bottom come the spring.

After so many years' practice Ivan can look at a hedge and easily tell where one man left off and another started. And with so many hedge-laying competition wins (notably the Coape-Arnold Cup) to his credit, he is the ideal judge of others.

Traditionally each competitor is given half a chain (33 feet) of hedge to lay in four hours. 'And he's got to do the lot *and* join the next man properly!' In normal work Ivan reckons on doing about a chain a day. 'You hear 'em talking about two chain a day, but I've never seen it yet. It's a job you can't rush, and should never be spoilt by things like putting string along the top. Once I laid a mile, but that took from November to March, and another time I did a quarter mile from 29 May to 12 August in me spare time. On my eightieth birthday I did half a chain from 10am to 2pm, and still managed an hour playing darts in the Sun!'

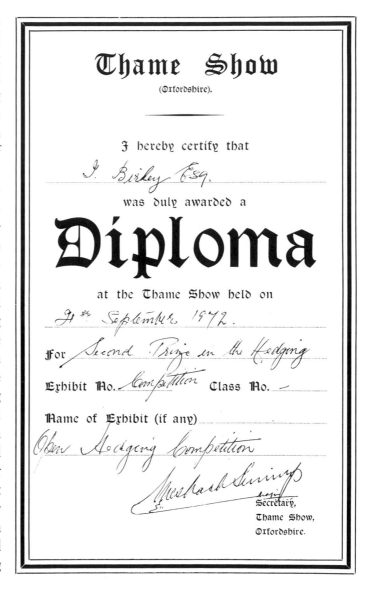

Hedges are not generally laid before attaining a height of at least six feet, but the height at which they are maintained thereafter varies considerably. 'If it's too tall, the wind will blow through and the stock won't like that, but if it's just right the wind goes over and by the time it's dropped back on the floor it's over the cattle. And I don't like to see trees in the middle of a hedge, but in the corner if some shade is required.'

The most awkward hedging which Ivan has laid is maple: 'horrible stuff, brittle as anything. Ash, wych-elm and elder are bad too. Whitethorn [hawthorn] and blackthorn are the best.'

Ivan's *Country File* – 'Small Green One' – award was given for organising and helping with the laying of about a mile of hedge which overhung the road adjoining the Berkshire, Buckinghamshire and Oxfordshire County Naturalists' Trust's Rushbeds Nature Reserve. The trust wanted it tidied in 'a wildlife-friendly way', so Ivan and a team of volunteers worked on it for two winters. Then Ivan decided to speed things up by holding a hedging competition, the thirty entrants coming from as far afield as Lancashire and Devon.

Ivan has also undertaken important work at the Bernwood Meadows Site of Special Scientific Interest, established to protect two flower-rich meadows and ancient hedgerows. There, a long blackthorn hedge is being successively cut over a long period to encourage regrowth. And even in his eighty-ninth year Ivan enthusiastically told me about his plans for further work there.

'…you had to catch 'em and hold 'em while the vet injected 'em.'

Ivan with his prize-winning heifer at Thame Fatstock Christmas Show in about 1970

Unfortunately, health, skill and willingness are not always enough. 'BBONT [the trust] said I couldn't instruct because I hadn't been on a course! After all these years I could only teach others by demonstration. Also, they couldn't get insurance for me to use a chainsaw over the age of eighty-five.'

Ivan has also had problems getting insurance for his scooter. 'I've had one for over thirty years and was with the Prudential, but they gave up bikes. I looked around, but nobody wanted to know on account of my age, but I've just found a company to take me on again. It's only a low-power scooter, but when I came out the army I had a Dunelt motorbike and in the 1940s an Enfield side-valve.'

In those days Ivan was on call twenty-four hours a day as a stockman:

If someone's dogs was chasin' sheep at 3am you had to get up and deal with it. It was hard work too, and I had many a kick off cows while milking. Before they invented the crush, when we was on TT [tuberculin testing], your milking cows was all chained up in stalls, but your youngstock – about a dozen two-year-old heifers – was in a loose-box and you had to catch 'em and hold 'em while the vet injected 'em. By the time you finished you couldn't see no clothes for muck.

But I got used to all that activity, which is why I got bored when I went to work for the Old Berkshire Hunt for a couple of years in the late 1950s. I lived at the kennels at Faringdon and had to open up jumps and mend gaps in hedges. I was always careful to pay my respects to the farmer before starting work and enjoyed what I did, but at night I had nothing to do.

In 1948 Ivan started showing sheep, cattle and beef carcasses at Thame Show, and he is still a steward on sheep there. But there have been years when things went wrong:

> We always showed a lamb carcass, with varying success. One year we had a late lamb and it didn't get a prize as it was too fat. But I thought I'd bid for it when it came to the auction, because it was meat you could really taste before it was even cooked. But to my surprise my boss bid for it, too, and ended up buying his own lamb for £15! The thing is, you weren't allowed to withdraw any animal from sale.
>
> Another time at auction my boss's nephew accidentally bought his uncle's heifer for 150 guineas. They'd seen this wool millionaire mark £150 next to it in his catalogue, and arranged that the nephew should stop bidding when uncle took his cigar out his mouth. But it all went wrong, and there was the boss's wife moaning at having to pay the auctioneer's £10 fee on top. But I pointed out that it was money well spent, as people would now know what good cattle we had.

Ivan's father only lived to the age of sixty-eight, but Ivan himself remains remarkably fit and active for his age, having already survived his wife Peggy by fourteen years. Apart from his hedge-laying (including frequent instruction of others), he still keeps an allotment, and he has been a regular beater, with his dog Jane, on the local Boarstall shoot for over thirty years. He was dominoes champion at the local Red Lion, and individual darts champion at the Royal Oak at the age of seventy-three, and he still enjoys a game of 'arrows'!

However, this accomplished father of four has some regrets. He says: 'Brill is more of a dormitory village now, with only about 25 per cent of the original villagers left. Most of the rest are incomers, either retired businessmen or people who work right away in London and other places. Also, today's farms are such miserable, quiet places, unlike the old days when everyone helped out with the harvest and there was always a horse and cart taking a load of kids out for lots of fun.' But whatever farms generally have become, there is no doubt that at least some have been considerably enriched through the vitality and competitive spirit of Ivan Birley.

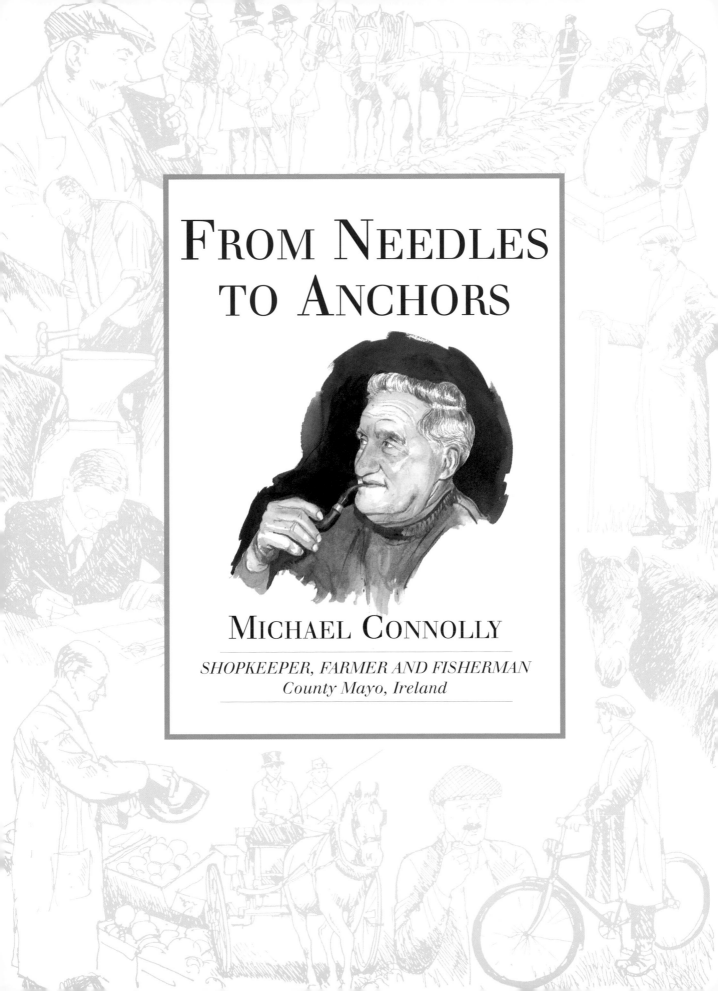

FROM NEEDLES TO ANCHORS

MICHAEL CONNOLLY

SHOPKEEPER, FARMER AND FISHERMAN
County Mayo, Ireland

As a shopkeeper in one of the most remote corners of western Ireland, with the sea never far away and transport always slow, Michael Connolly once had to provide customers with 'everything from needles to anchors'. And many other things which could not be ordered from distant towns were harvested locally from land and sea. Even now, many years later, his refreshingly wild and isolated part of Mayo demands a high degree of self-sufficiency. Michael still values the travelling library's fortnightly visit to Rossport, its DIY books having enabled him to carry out all the maintenance required on his house. And its educational works were instrumental in his gaining third place and a prize of £100 in a writing competition organised by Mayo County Council.

One of eight children, Michael Joseph Connolly was born on 15 August 1923 at Stonefield, Carrowteige, on the peninsula neighbouring Rossport. He recounts his family's early history:

My ancestors were driven here, from their lands east of the Shannon, by Cromwell's army, and the cry was: 'To hell, or Connaught'. After they settled, all lands, fishing rights and so on, were given to English landlords, with the result that, to this day, the people of the area, for the most part, have to emigrate to survive.

The first Connolly in these parts had to flee his native Galway because of his activities. He was known as a 'hedge' schoolmaster because the English banned teaching, which he had to carry on behind hedges or ditches to escape detection. Later, when teaching was legalised, he taught in a school at Carrowteige and his salary was just £12 a year.

The celebration of Mass was also prohibited, but that, too, was celebrated in isolated places, and very often a large rock was used instead of an altar. Hence the term 'Mass rock' in several places throughout Ireland.

Michael's grandfather was a fisherman and farmer who never left home, but his father was far more restless: 'He fished from the age of sixteen, mainly for lobsters, before going away to work in Scottish mines. Then he went to the States where he gathered a few bob on the trams, which enabled him to come back and start the shop at Stonefield. But I don't know whether Mum and Dad married in the States or here.'

Michael's very earliest memory is of clinging to his father's shoulders while out swimming. 'We were only fifty yards from the shore, but I thought we were half-way to America! I started bawling, but thankfully it didn't stop my love of the sea.'

Another memory from that time shows just how isolated the community was. When young Michael drank half a bottle of Sloane's Linament the doctor had to come twenty miles to revive him! But he was soon up and about, helping his father to fish for the pot. He remembers these days vividly:

Sometimes we'd empty the water from rockpools to get the small fish which frequented them. Later, in my early teens, while fishing around remote islands, myself and a few pals would sometimes be put ashore to collect birds' eggs for cake-making. And on spring tides father used to take huge crabs from the rocks. He had to insert his arm full-length into a hole barely wide enough to extract a crab. I was never too keen on this as a big crab would almost crush the bone if he got his claw around it. Many years ago a man was unable to extract his arm, and drowned when the tide rose. The crab holes were at or near low water and far away from the villages, so any cries for help would not be heard. Until about five years ago crabs were very plentiful – I've seen up to a hundred taken from a French barrel pot; but then there was no great demand for them. Now you would have to go about ten miles from the coast to get any crabs.

The traditional curragh is light and easy to carry

The Connollys' craft was the traditional curragh, a boat like an elongated coracle, of which there are at least four different types in Ireland. Michael still fishes a curragh he helped to build, and insists that it is one of the safest boats ever made:

Without a keel, it rides the sea the same as a seagull, and it takes a lot of wind to upset one. You should see the seas them old boats cut through. The biggest curraghs were some 22 feet long and had four men rowing with one steering. Each man had one 12-foot oar, 4 x 3 inches pared down at the blade. These were usually only ordinary white deal, but in those days the timber was much better. Smaller curraghs, used for lighter work, were propelled by paddles, three pairs at times.

Because the traditional curragh is built very light, it comes into its own where there are no piers and it has to be carried to safety. To make it we generally used hazel rods about five feet long and the thickness of a broom handle. They were softened with hot water or steam so they could be bent to fit into holes bored into the main frame, which could be any handy light timber. But nowadays access to the shore is often easier, and a lot of oak is used for frames because many people are more concerned that the wood should be long-lasting rather than light.

Michael Connolly baling out his curragh, which he helped to build

The 'skin' of the curragh used to be made from calico, which was available everywhere, and you sewed it down the centre to get the width. This was treated with Stockholm tar [prepared from resinous pinewood] which was the best, but later we had to use ordinary coal tar mixed with pitch which came in blocks and had to be boiled for an hour or more. You would drop a little on a stone and rub a wetted finger on it. If it didn't stick it was ready for applying.

Michael was among sixty to seventy children at Carrowteige National School, but he is not sure when he went there; he thinks he was probably around five or six years old. He describes those early years:

In those days many children went part-time because they had to help with the farm work and other things. But I was not that mad for school, anyway. Our family had about eighty sheep on the common ground and I often had to mind them. There were no wires then, and the fences only came when the commonage was split up among the owners. So us boys also had to mind that the cows didn't get into the potatoes.

We ate well at home, but mainly plain food. We fattened our own pig and hung the bacon in the rafters, but it was mostly fish and lots of potatoes – we loved them then, and we love them yet! The sandy soil makes for wonderful spuds here. I used to take the potatoes from the field, put them in a hole in the ground, cover them with sand and build a fire on top using drift-wood. Delicious! And with the fish I always liked the wrasse best, even though it has little commercial value. Just plain boil it fresh, or leave it overnight with salt on.

Young Connolly went fishing at every opportunity, sometimes with home-made rods fash-ioned from a broom handle, cane or hazel. And on the rivers he used a spillet, a long line with bent safety-pins baited with worms to catch small eels. Other boyhood games and pastimes included feats of strength, running and jumping; Michael recollects them clearly:

We had a ball made from roots torn from the sand and bound with twine. Another was a pig's bladder blown up. You wouldn't kick it very far against the wind!

Local houses were lit with oil lamps, then later paraffin. Water was easily obtained from the many spring wells in the area, and most people had a tank to catch the rain. Us kids often washed in the sea.

There was a lot of thatch then. Turfs about as big as a rug were laid over the rafters, which never had nails in, and covered with mainly rye straw as it was so tough. Most people thatched their own cottages, and later on I did hayricks, too.

Heating was always by peat and a little bog wood. One house I knew had no proper chim-ney, only a stone fireplace with the smoke coming out into the room and rising up through a hole in the roof when it wanted to. The seats on either side of the hearth were huge stones. This cottage was just one big room about 25 feet long, with the kitchen at one end and four or five cows at the other. The bed was right next to the fire and the horse was near the bed. The floor was rough stone, not even good flag, and there was no attic. The walls were 18-inch-thick

'And with the fish I always liked the wrasse best…'

'Another ball was a pig's bladder blown up.'

stone held together by gravel mortar with a bit of lime.

Most people were very poor, but very happy. It was all *maitheal* [joining together to get through the work]; I've seen as many as ten women around a frame stitching a bed quilt. But the women were always more at home than the men as superstition kept them away from the fishing. Nine or ten men would often gather round in a house, but usually only to talk. Ghost stories were a great thing then.

Local roads were very rough, being 'coarse gravel and one big problem. Even later, when they were tarred, it was always a bit worrying going to the side to let a lorry pass. It's ridiculous the huge vehicles they let on now. With the bog underneath the roads are always breaking up.

'I drove at ten in bare feet. Everyone was in bare feet then. I had a job to reach the clutch, but you didn't have to worry about indicators! Later on, when I was eighteen, we put on a taxi service, which was big business then with lots of people going away to pull beet in England, mostly May to October.'

As the coast is so indented in that area it was often quicker to go by boat across an estuary rather than travel all the way around by land. In any case, many parts were without proper roads. Michael recounts the many details of local life:

Up here there were two brothers who were full-time ferrymen. The priest used to come by boat and there was always a horseman to meet him.

Bodies, too, were ferried around by boat, the one cemetery being used by four or five villages, each with about twenty-five dwellings. Coffins were always carried on shoulders: there were *men* around at that time! Bodies were hardly ever taken to church as it was too far; they'd be waked in the house, with the usual load of tobacco and clay pipes, which the men often left on the ground. And there was always the home-brew poteen, as there were no pubs nearer than McGrath's, right round the estuary.

My old man was fairly keen on the poteen. Potatoes are often used to make it, but the handiest way is with molasses, treacle and sugar. Over near Ballycastle they had beautiful stuff made from barley. It was matured for at least six to twelve months, and had such a rich smell. Nothing like it now. Poteen should always be put through less than a gallon an hour, the final run just like a silk thread. Before the pubs started up in the area, myself and a friend borrowed the equipment to produce our own poteen, as you couldn't be sure of the quality of the stuff you would buy.

Just after the war you could hardly get good whiskey, but I had another source of drink. Spanish trawlers, about a couple of hundred ton each, used to fish in pairs near here. They had agents at Ballyglass, and when they radioed in to say they were coming in with fish for a fortnight I'd be there to meet them. I bought their brandy for only 10s [50p] a bottle, and sold it for good profit. But they robbed us of fish. I've seen them leaving Ballyglass with cod and other species all over the deck, and only an inch of freeboard.

When Michael's father first started the shop he, too, was dependent on the sea for transport:

He began by collecting two tons of supplies at a time by curragh. And it was really hard work once a fortnight, unloading with no pier and hauling along rough tracks. After that he travelled the twenty-five miles by road to Belmullet by horse and cart. Then he used a sailing boat, and in 1927 bought his first truck.

I was very lucky, and had access to everything in the shop, from sweets to Woodbines, and there wasn't much we didn't carry. We kept everything from cart grease and horseshoes to farm implements and turf spades. And if we didn't stock it, we'd soon order it; but it was a long time before the commercial travellers started to come round and make life easier. Towards the end we even did undertaking, using coffins made by local tradesmen and fittings that Father stocked.

The shop kept 'everything from Woodbines to cart grease'

We had about ten chests full of tea in the attic, and you always had to put out three or four for the old women, to see which ones they liked the look of. Even the worst of it then was better than the dust you get now. Sugar, too, came in large quantities – 2cwt sacks – and putting it in small bags was one of my jobs.

Michael left his mainly Irish-speaking school at the age of fourteen, and worked in the shop when he could be spared from the family farm. He soon learnt the art of patience: 'Customers very seldom paid immediately, and when they did it was often with eggs, grain or meat rather than money. But sometimes people had a few bob from good fishing or making poteen. And very nearly everyone had somebody in the States then, so the postman would be closely watched for a few dollars.'

When World War II came along, Michael spent three years as a coastal watcher. He describes what this involved:

It was fairly well paid, but the beauty for me was going away on training courses, to Galway and Athlone. Each lookout post was numbered and there were three or four between here and Belmullet. We had wonderful binoculars and telescopes, but the convoys were so far out all you saw were the masts. However, you could see the Flying Fortresses circling, with lost Yanks in, trying to read the post numbers to help find their way home.

Very few German planes passed, and there was little action in the area. But I do remember when the liner *Andorra Star* was torpedoed; it was carrying German and Italian prisoners-of-war, and several of their bodies came ashore here. The two biros found on them were the first ever seen in this area! I also got part of a lifeboat with the name on it, tins of biscuits, two or three big tins of coffee and loads of other things. I was coming home on wings to tell them about it!

Michael moved to his present home, at Rossport, shortly after he married Eva in 1952.

Her parents lived next door, and her uncle offered us this house. I had a truck then, and my business was general haulage of peat to Ballina and bringing stuff back, anything and everything from pigs to wardrobes. I travelled up to about sixty miles.

Peat around here is the very best and has always been in demand. On my patch I'm now down about ten feet, into the second cutting. There are at least several feet more, but then you get the problems with water run-off. When the machines came in they could deal with all the tough places the people had neglected. The peat is sold in boxes by the ton, usually three- to five-ton loads. Now [1994] a trailer load about 10 feet long, 7 feet wide and 6 feet high costs up to £90 locally, and we'd have about six loads in a year. When I was a boy the cheapest was about £7 a load. It's sometimes sold by the stack, but then the quantity's a bit of guesswork.

In about 1960 Michael and a few other men bought a 32-foot half-decker and fished it for about three years, mainly on lobsters and crayfish. But as Michael pointed out, 'it was very difficult due to the lack of proper piers, and very dangerous due to the treacherous coastline and the lack of other boats in the area at the time. The nearest lifeboat station then was sixty miles away, so if anything went wrong, one hadn't much hope of rescue.' He continues:

Then, 26-foot boats became available, and I fished them for a few years, mainly on salmon and lobsters. I gave up commercial fishing in 1975 to work a small farm as my family had moved out. I still fish for the pot with my 18-foot curragh, sometimes with my wife. Pollack and wrasse are the main catch, with the odd summer sea-trout and lobster.

When we were kids and forever bathing, at least in summer, you would sometimes hear a shout where someone had stepped on a plaice. Of course the tendency was to jump off, but after a while some of us learnt to press down, and sometimes we caught a good-sized fish. And dabs and flounders were plentiful in the estuaries as late as the 1970s.

But the fishing's nothing like it was. On a good day I've had as many as twenty flatfish in a few hours fishing with lugworm; now, there is hardly one left. In the old days, too, you could almost go out with a bucket and lift the salmon, there were so many. And the mackerel shoals would nearly blind you with their phosphorescence; the sea would almost take off with them.

The increase in seals and over-fishing's only half the problem. I always loved beachcombing and used to get lots of strange wood, weed, coconuts and other things which must have come from South America. But in the last five years there's not been one bit of this, and my theory is that the Gulf Stream has changed course, resulting in a colder sea and poorer inshore fishing. This used to be one of the richest fishing grounds in Europe. Four of us in a 26-footer once got six thousand mackerel in a day with only handlines and jigs. And I can remember fifty English steam [coal] trawlers out here in the bay at one time.

When they weren't protected, we used to get a bounty of £1, which later rose to £2, for a seal's head, though we actually sent in only the noses because of the size. I've counted at least twenty-five salmon taken from my nets by seals in one day, and the bits they leave are quite unsaleable. So I always used to shoot them at every chance I had. I wouldn't like to do away with them completely, but I do think they should be controlled. There's all these rich folk here in the winter with their chargers chasin' the foxes for *fun*, but we're not supposed to shoot the seals, and that's our living!

We also shot the cormorant, for a bounty of ten shillings. There used to be every kind of wildlife here, but now there's only about 25 per cent left. But at least we still have the brent geese, and plenty of otters, which take no notice of me.

Michael still gathers the local shellfish, but only for home consumption. Among them are mussels, cockles, winkles, clams and several others whose English names he does not know. Among his favourites are limpets, which he puts through the mincer after boiling.

He also harvests the seaweed, 'the long, flat, black, slimy variety which can be reached at low water. I used to sell it by the thirty-ton load. It was in great demand for baths, which people would pay to visit. And in the war it was used when bandages were short. They also noticed that it helped to cure wounds, but the big drug companies wouldn't want to hear that! I found the seaweed excellent for my arthritic elbow; it cured it in two weeks, but it did colour my arm a bit. I always rub it on my face for shaving – it's better than any soap, as the Japanese know. That's why I have such good skin. And sometimes I have a bath with it.' When Michael does so, Eva says 'he has so much seaweed in there you can just see his head poking out like a seal. It makes the bath a bit brown, but he really believes in it!'

Michael has also sampled 'dulse', seaweed which is generally eaten when dried and sells for about 25p per ounce. 'Another, called "slouk" or "slowk" – *sloucan* in Irish – is eaten after cooking, and was once in great demand for export.'

Another local wild product which is still harvested and commonly sold in shops is Carrageen moss. 'Nowadays people mostly take it for their chests and to make custard, but in the old days we chiefly fed it to young calves to make their coats shine.'

But even without the help of seaweed and such a healthy natural diet, I think Michael Connolly would have a fine glow to his skin because he lives in such an invigorating area. The friendliness of the local people was most apparent when I stayed at nearby McGrath's Inn, which has been in the same family for centuries. There, too, the spirit of independence and self-sufficiency remains strong.

As I supped my first pint of stout at McGrath's, the landlord's son came in from the sleety gale cradling a weak, newborn lamb which needed urgent treatment. Later that evening tables and chairs were quickly moved aside and a curtain drawn across one end of the bar when the local 'keep fit' class arrived. But then there was just a little rivalry as the music accompanying the unseen, energetic fitness pupils competed with the ever-increasing volume of the now almost universal bar television. In front of the Guinness and Smithwick's pumps, a row of proud heads, most of them speaking Irish, angled up and sideways, determined to hear the wise words of their lady president. All seemed content to watch the world from afar.

'How is the lamb?' I asked Mrs McGrath the landlady as she relaxed with me by the fire. 'Dead!' she proclaimed without a flicker of emotion. But then she had only just returned from her fifth funeral in one week, such is the strength of the local community. And I was not too surprised, either, when she told me that when she went to London she did not have time to see any sights at all because she had so many relatives and friends to visit! 'I didn't want to offend anyone.'

The everyday lives and adventures of the local people have long provided rich subject matter for traditional song, a great interest of Michael's. He has composed several ballads in English and Irish, some of which have been sung by his son on the Irish language radio station, Radio na Gaeltachta, on which Michael, too, has broadcast.

Two of the Connollys' sons live in Galway, but the third and their only daughter live in southern England, in very contrasting surroundings. Yet while their lives there may be more exciting or provide more lucrative employment, far greater natural treasures remain in their homeland.

In his soft western voice, Michael summed up his feelings as we strolled along the shore at the bottom of his long garden. 'Would you believe me when I say I actually cried one morning when I came down here to lift the nets. The sun was just coming up, everything was all rose-tinted, and I thought of my son away in London, and all that he was missing.'

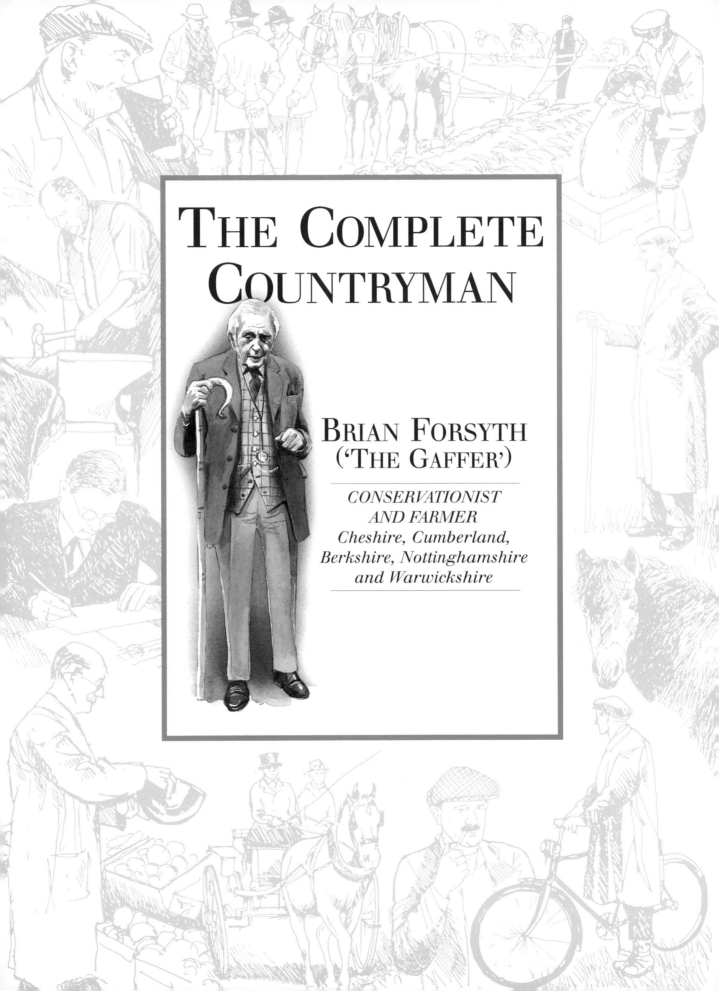

THE COMPLETE COUNTRYMAN

BRIAN FORSYTH ('THE GAFFER')

CONSERVATIONIST AND FARMER

Cheshire, Cumberland, Berkshire, Nottinghamshire and Warwickshire

Whether by constraint or desire, the lives of most countrymen revolve around only a small number of professional and leisure activities. Furthermore, the majority have their fields of interest clearly mapped out by strong family association. But just once in a while along comes a man with such great energy and enthusiasm for the outdoors that he becomes closely involved in almost every area of country life. One such man is ninety-year-old Brian Forsyth who, despite having a father whose life centred on the sea, can justifiably claim to be the complete countryman. Not only has he established a highly successful farming business, he has also won a major conservation award, and is one of the greatest champions of almost every country sport. Often outspoken but ever a gentleman, he despises social barriers and is passionate in the defence of traditional village and country life. He may believe that he has seen the best of England, but, unlike Britain's ever-increasing army of 'armchair conservationists', he is actively fighting for all he has cherished.

The eldest and last surviving of three brothers, Brian George Tyrer Forsyth was born at Wallasey, Cheshire, on 20 October 1905. Of Scottish descent, most of his forebears, including the Tyrer-Forsyths of Cheshire and Lancashire, farmed or went to sea. In Brian's own words:

> Grandad Law on mother's side did damn all, except sailing, until he lost all his money. And Dad's father didn't do much either. But my father was in shipping all his life, at Liverpool, where he managed the John Herron line of cargo boats.
>
> When I was two years old we moved some ten miles south to a country house at Heswall, which was our home for thirty years.

Schoolboy Brian (right) and his family in about 1912 at Westlands, Heswall, where they lived for thirty years

One of my very earliest memories is from World War I, when I went down to the docks with Father to see one of his ships come in with Canadian horses for the war effort. The skipper was really bleary-eyed after the arduous crossing, and the first thing he said to Father was: 'I started with six hundred horses and I've still got six hundred', which was a great achievement in those days. But I noticed that the horses were up to their bellies in muck in open stalls, some on deck, and when I queried it the captain told us they were like this so that if they rolled over in a rough sea – which they'd had plenty of – they wouldn't hurt themselves.

When the Herron ships passed Dad's office they always blew their foghorns to let him know they were home safe and sound. But there could also be considerable danger on land and the dock police had to go about in pairs for protection against thugs. One of them told me about the time a cargo boat came in without rat cups on the ropes. As he approached it he suddenly saw such a large swarm of rats coming towards him that he legged it as fast as he could.

My uncle was the chairman of the cotton exchange in Liverpool, and one day he showed me the derringer he always carried in his pocket. 'I really needed that when I was in America', he said.

It was an altogether more friendly and pleasant environment where the Forsyths lived, out in the countryside overlooking the Dee estuary, 'then a wildfowler's paradise'. To hear the wild geese flying over on a moonlit night, 'honking and making a noise like a pack of hounds in full cry', is something which has always thrilled Brian, both in childhood and old age. Inland, in those early days, Brian fondly recalls the beauty of the natural countryside:

There was a corncrake in every field, and if you walked into a field of meadow grass, butterflies and moths of every colour and description rose in clouds. Orchids were everywhere, and the summer hawthorn hedges were always covered with dust as there were no metalled roads.

Father earned about £1,000 a year, which I suppose was a lot then, but he sent all three of us boys to public school and we never seemed to have that much money. We had two maids who were paid damn all, but lived in, and a woman to do the washing. I can never remember Mother doing much work. Our jobbing gardener came one day a week and earned half-a-crown.

We lived between the upper and lower village, where there was a lot of thatch, down by the estuary. In the village shop they'd just put a hand in the jar and grab the sweets you wanted, but it didn't kill us. It's all too fussy nowadays. At one place I knew, the bedroom was the shop and the old girl who ran it slept on the double bed in the corner! That was at Caergwrle, near Wrexham, which we visited when we went on holiday to our wonderful grandparents' cottage at Hope. We could never go very far during the war years as Father always had to be near his office.

Gradually people started to move out from Liverpool, but they had no cars and mostly had to travel to work by train. In the evenings there were always six horse-drawn cabs by the station. One was driven by an ancient man in a top hat and you paid him a shilling to go most places, or two shillings if it was very far. If you wanted a cab you just put your hand up and he acknowledged you by raising his whip.

The men who commuted from the country were all immaculately dressed. On the Birkenhead ferry across to Liverpool they'd all be up on deck in their bowlers taking the air. And whenever Father went to London he always wore a frock-coat and top hat.

Brian remembers the day, in 1912, when the first car was seen in the village:

My brothers and I were out with our maid, Fanny, when suddenly we heard this *chug chug chug*, gradually getting louder. There were traps drawn up on both sides of the street and all the ponies started snorting, so their owners had to rush out to hold their heads. Then the car – I think it was a de Dion Bouton or a Renault – came into view, steered by a tiller, the driver with goggles, cap and muffler.

Transport must have been very bumpy and unpleasant then because the roads were just earth and stones, mostly taken from the shore, and they were very muddy in winter and white with dust in summer. Near us there used to be an old man with wire-mesh glasses who sat on a sack and chipped away at rocks for the road for days on end.

Unusual for the time, we had a telephone, which Father needed to keep in touch with shipping movements; he also had a damn great code book for it, during the first war.

We made our own pleasures then. Cards was always the great thing in the evenings, especially among farming people and after a day's shooting. When film shows started you had to take a train to reach the picture house. So there was a lot of time for reading and letter writing. Sadly, the art is mostly gone now.

Brian was first educated at St Fillan's Preparatory School. 'It was run by an old girl in a house down by the shore. Although it was two miles away we walked there and back twice a day, totalling eight miles, so that we could go home for lunch. And on a Sunday you went for a walk after tea in the summer and before tea in the winter. But you thought nothing of it then. That's why I'm walking now.'

Next came a period at the local Mostyn House School, Parkgate:

It was run by Dr Grenfell, whose brother was the first man to explore Labrador and who invented the famous Grenfell watercloth. It was while I was there, during World War I, that I saw my first plane, a biplane which crashed nearby.

At school you could be either a 'wet bob' or a 'dry bob'; I hated cricket, so became a 'wet bob' and took up sailing. For safety you wore a ring round your neck or a kapok waistcoat, and at thirteen or fourteen years of age I became proficient in rough seas.

I loved the coast, and went barefoot before Wellingtons came in at 10s a pair, then thigh boots at £1. The local fishermen had leather thigh boots which were coated in grease to keep them supple, but they smelt like hell. One of the old salts was Spurner Smith. Us lads used to go into his immaculate, clean cottage to listen to his tales of the sea. Occasionally he caught rare fish, and said: 'I don't know the name of it but it's good to eat!' So we ate them too, and they were always delicious.

When the boats came in laden with plaice, dabs and other fish the fishermen's wives went down to meet them. They put white cloths on their heads to carry heavy baskets of fish – so fresh they were almost still flapping – up to about three miles to sell them. They'd come to our back door, to the tradesmen's entrance – never to the front – and be taken inside. In those days we had a kitchen, a back kitchen, a scullery, pantry and larder, and the fisherwomen always set their baskets down in the scullery. There you'd pick the fish you wanted, and the women would gut them and take their heads off. Then you knew they were really fresh fish.

At the harvest festival of the sea, the fishermen hung their nets up in the chapel and brought in fish and shrimps on plates. They always boiled their shrimps alive as soon as they came in.

Like many other country lads, Brian was a keen collector of birds' eggs, butterflies and moths, for which he bought a killing jar from the local chemist. 'Its bottom was thick with a special paste, and I also had a cork setting board. I always remember how excited we all were when I caught a death's head hawk-moth in the garden. I still have it somewhere. Also there was this place with acres of nettles which was a haven for moths. Torches had only just come in, so at first we went out holding a lantern with a candle in, or a paraffin lamp. One night we were having such a marvellous time we stayed out very late, and got into terrible trouble at home!'

Coarse fishing was another favourite pastime, at first with simple cane and string. 'Then we went to Monk's of Chester, and I bought a 9ft greenheart rod and a Hardy reel. And later I had one of those wonderful Hardy guides, which have now become collectors' items. I used to stay with a friend who had a huge pond, and he taught me how to handle perch without getting their spikes into my hand.'

A less orthodox form of fishing was learnt when Brian was at prep school and some-times stayed at Llandrillo millhouse, in Wales. 'Cadwallader, the miller, used to say to me:

'Cards was always the great thing in the evenings . . .'

On the day in 1912 when the first car was seen in their village: Brian (left), his two younger brothers and their maid Fanny

"The bailiff's away. Come with me and we'll get some trout". So we would wade in with bare feet, and hit about six trout with a stick. It was very easy as the water was so shallow, we just went wonk on their heads; but we didn't take any little fish.'

Shooting was another of Brian's great loves:

I started getting rabbits with snares, and then graduated to a Daisy airgun. Then Father took me to Monk's and bought me a single-barrel 28-bore shotgun. I remember the first rabbit I killed with it. The very first morning I had the gun I got up early and just walked down the hedge, without asking permission. I was so pleased with my shot, and took the rabbit home for the maid to skin and cook.

I suppose I poached that rabbit, but in those days anyone who took just one or two for the pot didn't get into much trouble as there were far fewer people. Many years ago I was out hedge-laying with an old poacher and at one point said to him, 'We'll be running into a rabbit warren in a minute'. 'Don't you worry, I'll deal with that,' he said. 'I wondered what was moving in your pocket,' I replied when I saw his ferret.

We also shot all sorts of birds in the old days, including waders such as dunlin, golden plover and redshank. Dunlin pie was marvellous.

Nobody minded if you walked into the village with a gun under your arm. Unlike today when everyone wants to see your gun open for safety, I always carried mine unbroken then, because a keeper once gave me such a clip for carrying my gun open. He said I'd damage the lock.

There were plenty of bobbies on the beat then in every village, and one day when I was off shooting, one of them said to me: 'If you've a duck when you come back, I'd be glad of it'. And he was.

Policemen never stood any nonsense then. One day I met this kid crying and he said that the same bobby I'd given the duck to had clipped him round the ear with his kid gloves, which they always carried on their belt in those days. The policeman told him: 'It's not for what you've done but what you might do!'.

Later, Brian acquired a secondhand, hammerless Westley Richards 12-bore for £10 in Liverpool. 'But it was too heavy for me and I never shot well with it, so in my old age I changed to a lighter 16-bore. But I didn't like that either, so I went back to a 28-bore, a double, and got on well with it. Then I tried a double four-ten. Now I've given all my guns to my grandchildren as there are too many restrictions today. Willie still has my Belgian single four-ten bought for £1 10s in 1912.'

In 1915 Brian's father took him to Lowther sheepdog trials, where they saw the famous 'Yellow Earl', the Earl of Lonsdale, one of the greatest sportsmen of the century. 'Behind him walked the countess and six elegant ladies who were his girlfriends. Then came his groom leading his cob, just in case he needed it. Behind them were two open, horse-drawn carriages; on the back of each was a "tiger", a boy groom with arms folded, whose job it was to jump down and open doors, and there was also a postilion riding the near horse of each pair. All were decked out in the earl's light-brown livery. It was a wonderful sight. And as they passed, the earl stopped to speak to every farmer and shepherd. He was very popular and they all called him "Lordy" behind his back.'

Another distinctively dressed man of the time was Heswall's Canon Dickie May. 'He wore a huge, broad-brimmed black hat, black silk waistcoat, breeches and gaiters, and as he walked through the village the little boys would pull their forelocks and the little girls would curtsy. But the vicarage had a long drive lined with chestnut trees and poor old Canon May had to run the gauntlet of the rookery there, with all the sticks and droppings raining down white on his black clothes.

'I loved the noise of that rookery. It was so soothing. Many years later, here in Warwickshire, I was so sad when Dutch elm disease took about six hundred of our trees as I'd managed to get the rooks' nests in them up from only two to eleven.'

When he was fifteen, Brian left Mostyn School to board at St Bees, near Whitehaven, on the Cumberland coast. He remembers his school and college days very well:

When it was time to leave for St Bees I started to cry, but Mother, who was a very Edwardian lady with long dress sweeping down the steps, slapped my wrist and said: 'Stop it. You're British and don't you forget it, and be proud of it.' But at least while I was away Father started to send me *Shooting Times* magazine, which I've taken ever since.

St Bees took 125 boys then, but now there are 200 as well as 200 girls. It was very remote, in a place where it was easy to become a duck poacher; it took all day to get there by train. Coming home at the end of term we had special carriages which took us to London, and on them we drank sherry and threw toilet rolls out the windows till the whole train was festooned with them. But this stopped when the railway people had too much of it. Now I have seven grandchildren at boarding school and they all come home at weekends. In our day many boys never saw their parents from one holiday to the next, though mine usually came up mid-term.

Brian (right) at St Bees School in the early 1920s

I left school in 1923. I'd wanted to farm and hunt, shoot and fish from the moment I could talk, so I decided to study agriculture at college. But before I went I was required to have practical experience, so Father paid £125 a year for my keep on a farm at Bunbury, in Cheshire. The farmer had a really good deal because I had to work like hell, just as hard as the men he paid.

Some mornings ten of us milked a hundred cows by hand, and it was my job to carry all the milk off, using a yoke with a four-gallon bucket at each end, which half killed your shoulders. In those days we also used to carry two-hundredweight sacks on our backs. Now they're not even a hundredweight, but we were taught how to lift and carry, and there weren't the bad backs like today.

In 1924 there was a bad outbreak of foot and mouth disease and the ministry employed butchers to kill all the cattle and pigs on the farm. The carcasses were then burnt and at night you could see all the fires on the different farms in the area. I was put on at £3 10s a week to scrape down and wash and disinfect the walls and tidy up generally. The farmers were compensated and I went with my boss to Penrith market, where we stayed the night, to buy replacement cows. But before he bought any he made me milk them to make sure their teats and udders were in good order.

The experience at Bunbury enabled Brian to attend Reading University, which received its charter while he was there, in 1925–6:

Reading was a beautiful town then, full of trams and very smart horses and carriages. I was in digs and had just ten bob pocket money, but we had a lot of fun, such as when we tied two trams together and scarpered, and the time when I let a mouse out in a botany lecture and caused chaos with the lady tutor. My great pal was Jack Houghton-Brown. I never saw him again, but, by huge coincidence, many years later his son became a friend of my son when they were both farming in Warwickshire. Then I discovered that Jack and I had both achieved our ambitions to become big farmers, and be able to hunt and shoot.

Oxford bags came in when I was at Reading. We went to the tailor and chose our own cloth for £1 a pair, but when I left I had them cut down and made much narrower in the country style.

After university, Brian went home to the Wirral Peninsula, to work for Ralph Leech at Landicam Farm, near Birkenhead, where he received his keep and 7s 6d a week. There he gained further experience in milking cows and driving horses, although the farm had two early tractors.

Then, again to increase his knowledge, Brian went to a farm near Worksop, where he received £1 a week and his keep. But he did not stay there long when he found out that his main job was to drive the owner from pub to pub in a huge Daimler with open gate-change gears; he was used to a little Austin 7. He describes how his life took a different turn:

With my brother I started keeping poultry in Cheshire. We established the Tyrer Pedigree Poultry Farm and sold eggs for the table and for sitting. By then, Dad was chairman of the first Wirral and District Council and had decided to retire from shipping. He, too, went into farming, buying a small place which he later added to at Fenny Compton, in Warwickshire. Later we moved to Prior's Marston, Warwickshire, where we rented a bigger farm.

Being in farming and having a duodenal ulcer I was exempt from war service, so I became a special constable. One day we were having a course in the sergeant's house at Southam when great screams suddenly came from the kitchen. We all rushed out to help, but it was only a mouse on the floor by the sergeant's wife!

' . . . it was my job to carry all the milk off.'

When he was at Fenny Compton, Brian met 'a little blond', Sybil Wheildon, while out hunting:

I caught her horse for her, and after that we hunted a lot together. She lived here at Tubbs End Farm. During the war we married in that church there across the field and rented a cottage in Prior's Marston opposite the big farmhouse where my family lived and soldiers were billeted. We had no sanitation indoors, only a loo in the garden.

One night in the blackout we had army manoeuvres here, and when I heard the tanks and troops coming I opened the bedroom window and shone a torch out. Then a voice roared: 'Tell that silly bugger to put that light out!'

On our land the war left three bomb craters which had to be filled in. I vividly remember the end of the war, when they were sending the thousand-bomber raids out. We were surrounded by aerodromes so there was a tremendous noise as hundreds of planes left in the dusk. One Wellington bomber crashed near us and all the crew died in the flames. We were out hunting, but couldn't do anything to help. Officially there was no hunting in the war, but people tried to keep it going a bit to control the foxes.

After the war Brian's brother Keith decided to leave farming to go into commerce with their other brother:

> Sybil's father was the tenant of Christchurch College, Oxford, and Tubbs End was very run down, being graded by the 'War Ag' as a C farm. Mr Wheildon said he couldn't carry on, so when the agent from Christchurch went to see him he suggested that I was called in to help. So in 1947 I gave up my tenancy at Prior's Marston and entered into partnership with father-in-law.
>
> In the nineteenth century, Tubbs End Farm and the manor house employed fifteen people, including maids, gardeners and grooms, all from the village. But before World War II it was down to five men and a boy at Tubbs End. When I moved in, the big house had no electricity and no mains drainage, and the three-seater privy in the garden had spaces for one child, one teenager and one adult. Our water came from two wells in the field; they dried up in a drought one year, and then we had to get Leamington Fire Brigade out with their fuel bowser. On one night when they came, a tremendous thunderstorm broke while they were on the way, and there was a drenched fireman at the door saying: 'We've brought your water!' But we still took it.
>
> After a few years the old people [mother- and father-in-law] moved down here into this cottage, as I did later on to make way for my son and his family. It's always been known as the dower house. Incidentally, when father-in-law died he probably had one of the very last funerals where a farmer was taken to his grave on one of his own wagons. He lay in state at the house and we buried him at the local church just over there. The wagon was drawn by two horses and we all walked behind. That was still the tradition in the mid-1950s.

At this time Christchurch College became short of money and decided to sell Tubbs End, one of their six farms in the area; Brian and the other farmers were given first option, but were told that purchase could only proceed if they *all* agreed to buy. The price for Tubbs End's 300 acres was £14,000, and Brian was very worried about raising such a sum as farming was then in a bad way and his in-laws did not want to use their capital so late in life.

> The accountant advised me not to buy, and as it turned out it was a damn good thing I didn't. Three of the tenant farmers declined the offer, and the very next day Christchurch sold all six farms – together about 2,000 acres – to the Mercantile and General Reassurance Company for £45,000, along with us sitting tenants. Their chairman was Ken Goschen, who started his own pack of hounds, and we were very happy under him, as he really understood farming. But when he died the landlords were pin-striped and out of touch with country life. Then Mercantile sold out to a Wolverhampton company who applied for planning permission to convert farm buildings into houses. Fortunately they didn't get it, and when the estate came onto the open market my sons, who had already become very successful in farming, bought the lot. I gradually dropped out of things and stopped signing business cheques in my seventies.

However, retirement from business management did not mean that Brian would sit idly by watching his sons. On the contrary, he had already become very closely involved with other lifelong interests, one of these being conservation. A major achievement was that in 1983 he was given *Country Life* magazine's prestigious Farming and Wildlife Award, the Silver Lapwing Trophy; he had been a runner-up for this award in 1981. This was because he had clearly shown just how well modern agriculture can accommodate wildlife, trees and flowers yet remain highly profitable. Sadly, Sybil died a few months before it was announced, so never knew of the recognition bestowed on her husband.

Brian lived alone in his cottage until Janet Wicks, 'also a blond', walked back into his life and became his second wife, bringing with her a menagerie of five dogs, numerous ducks, peacocks and guinea fowls. 'We had known each other since she was nine years old.'

Apart from a little grazing, the Forsyths' land had concentrated on cereals and oilseed rape, and there were few natural habitats of value. Thus to win the Silver Lapwing Trophy from 150 entries as far apart as Scotland and Cornwall was a great achievement. Brian demonstrated that the monotonous, eerily silent 'prairie' landscapes normally associated with arable farming are not essential. However, his effort also showed that conservation certainly costs money on a large scale, through the provision of trees and considerable manpower and suchlike, and will continue only as long as a business can afford it.

Brian's interest in conservation began through his involvement in fieldsports; as he explains:

> When you shoot and hunt and start to look after game and their habitat you automatically start to help all the other birds and animals. Most of it is commonsense. But the Farming and Wildlife Advisory Group, of which I am a member, have been very helpful. I'm also a member of the British Association for Shooting and Conservation, the British Field Sports Society and the Game Conservancy, as well as the National Trust, the Country Landowners' Association, the Warwickshire Naturalists' Trust and the Royal Society for the Protection of Birds.
>
> Although I don't shoot now, my sons Anthony and James are very keen and I still enjoy beating and picking up on our family shoot. With the aid of our 85-year-old keeper, Teddy West, whose father was keeper to Lord Willoughby de Broke, we put down just enough birds to ensure five or six entertaining days each season. This provides the opportunity to repay the many invitations my sons get elsewhere, though the emphasis is very much on enjoyment rather than big bags.

With such great attention to habitat management on the farm, there is less reliance on release schemes. Much to the surprise of many people, Brian and Teddy also ensure that their land harbours a few foxes as well as pheasants. Brian stresses that 'it is possible to keep them both, but you mustn't kill a *resident* fox, otherwise a stranger will move in. Foxes have their own territory, and will not kill on their own doorstep. It is the hunting travelling fox which causes the damage.' So when the Forsyth elms were lost to disease, Brian put the wood to good use by creating a number of huge log-piles around the farms to provide places where the foxes could hole up and even breed. This great love of foxes is easy to understand, as Brian has hunted for most of his life.

There are, of course, plenty of hedgerows on Forsyth land, and these are kept to an A shape, 5ft high and 8–10ft through the bottom, to provide nest-sites for a wide variety of songbirds, 'some of which are very fussy about how deep in a hedge they will nest'. The shape also allows maximum light penetration to crops. Brian stresses that flail-cutting 'all depends on the man using the flail. We are proud of our hedges, which are cut by a young

Brian's land harbours foxes as well as pheasants

man with a keen eye. A good conservation hedge must be left high enough for birds to be able to get away from rats. Some farmers crucify their hedges with a flail, making them so tight and low they are nothing more than field boundaries.'

With cereals come huge sprayers and combines, and therefore the temptation to tear out whole hedgerows so that spraying and harvesting are made easier; but the Forsyths have got round this problem by providing hedge breaks of just sufficient width – some 45ft – to allow the bigger machines to get through. Furthermore, the family has both created and reinstated many hedgerows.

Where fields meet, farms often have sharp-angled corners; growing cereals in these is not economic, as the big machines cannot get in there easily, and crops may be excessively shaded. Much better to have a smooth border to each field and plant up those odd corners for the benefit of nature, as the Forsyths have done so successfully.

Brian also explained that their policy is to spray crops as little as possible, so as to give wildlife a better chance. 'And a lower dose on the right day is far better than a full dose on the wrong one. Without any spraying the crop would be a jungle, and we couldn't contemplate leaving an unsprayed strip around a field on this land as the worst weeds are next to the hedge. However, the one-yard-wide sterile strip we leave between hedge and crop not only prevents weeds from spreading into the crop, it also provides a corridor for game and other wildlife.' This is most important as it affords somewhere for birds, and especially chicks, to dry out and so avoid chilling, and this in turn will reduce the mortality rate. In addition, the Forsyths have experimented with letting the hedge grow out over the sterile strip to improve protection for birds against predators. The hedge itself still contains an abundance of chick food plants and insects, and the spray bar is totally enclosed by a shield to stop chemical drift.

The wealth of birdlife literally before Brian's window is a constant delight; here, many species come to be fed on and around an attractively laid out pond, once the site of a tip. Two species, however, the magpie and carrion crow, are not welcome there and have to be controlled. Brian stresses that if they did not shoot them regularly they would not have a single duck left on their pools or brook. 'It is heartbreaking to see a mallard swim into my pool with half a dozen ducklings, and within a few days the brood is reduced to one or two. The crows perch in the trees waiting for the ducklings to appear in open water and then take them in a swift swoop.'

Another predator whose numbers need to be kept in balance in today's manicured landscape is the fox. Each year Brian holds a lawn meet at Tubbs End Farm for the Warwickshire Foxhounds, who usually hunt on Forsyth land on about four days a season.

Brian is also a keen beagler, and holds a lawn meet for the Warwickshire Beagles. 'I got interested as a young man in the Wirral, cycling to meets of the Royal Rock – the oldest beagle pack in the country – and then following hounds on foot. In those days the huntsman drove an old cab with a horse and the hounds were in the back.

'I quite enjoy the social side of the sport, but for real hunting people the main thing is watching hounds work; personally I'm never bothered if we don't make a kill. I would say there are no bad days, it's only that some are better than others.'

To say that Brian remains passionate about hunting would be an understatement. His walls are covered with hunting pictures, his bookshelves are bulging with hunting books and his year is crammed with hunting days, often four a week! His old brown Range Rover is a familiar sight at meets throughout the country. Although the farm workshop struggles to keep it on the road, he would be lost without it because it has so many gadgets geared to his requirements. For example, he finds the doors very heavy so he has dog leads attached to them to help pull them to. But even with these accessories he does not like motorway travel and prefers to let someone else take over. 'The only way to go up the M6 is to have a good whisky, strap yourself in and go to sleep.'

Ever since he went to school there, Brian has regarded Cumberland as his second home. He still goes up there to hunt with six fell packs – 'whichever is the handiest' – about five times a year, and to judge terriers at important shows such as Rydal, Lowther and Borrowdale. But whereas once he favoured a good hotel, now he prefers the home comforts of a Borrowdale farmhouse.

Over many years in Cumberland Brian has befriended some remarkable country characters; one such was Jonty Hines, who died at eighty-two.

As a child, Jonty used to walk six miles over Honister Pass, along a very rough road, just for the chance to earn tuppence. He went to meet the coach, to take the 'slippers' off the back wheels; these 'slippers' were used as brakes when going downhill over shale and got very hot. Jonty was one of the boys who had the knack of wrapping a cloth around his hands, hooking the slippers off, dropping them into a bucket of water to cool off and hooking them back onto the coach.

Jonty was a retired quarryman, who had a very old house with a beautiful, early court cupboard built in. Wherever we went he seemed to know everybody, and would always say: 'Yon's me cousin, yon's me niece, yon's me uncle,' and so on. I met him in the bar of the Scafell Hotel, where even respectable visitors would be turned out of his seat.

One year when I was at Scafell, a boasting man in a Jaguar, who had no idea how many years I'd been going up there, asked me: 'How long did it take you to come up on the motorway?' But before I could reply, Jonty said to him: 'Nay lad, he's local; but he does own a big farm in Warwickshire.'

Another great Cumbrian character was the late Johnny Richardson, huntsman to the

Terriers remain an important part of the Forsyth household

Blencathra. I always remember one day in the mid-1980s when we were out with John Barnet, one of the Warwickshire joint-masters I'd been introducing to fell hunting. After a while John asked Johnny: 'How many hounds have you put on today?' Johnny replied in his broad drawl: 'I doown't know'. During the morning John put the same question three times, and each time he received the same answer. But four times was one too many, and Johnny turned round to John and said, rather more strongly: 'I dooown't know, but I tell you what, I'll know if there's ought missing!'

Brian earned the nickname 'Gaffer' when he was amateur terrierman to the Warwickshire Foxhounds, from 1970 to 1982. 'I suppose most of the followers had got used to me and one day somebody said to another: "Don't you do anything without asking the Gaffer". After that it just stuck, and over the years I've even written magazine articles as "The Gaffer", and a horse has been named after me.'

Dogs, and especially terriers, remain a prominent and important part of the Forsyth household, though some are more temperamental than others! Indeed, as Brian 'tuned in' to my questions he commented: 'I have to be very careful with my hearing aids now, as my terriers have eaten two of them!' Nevertheless, these are dogs for which he obviously has great respect and affection:

I've always worked terriers, mostly bolting foxes: they've been my life. We've had some remarkable days together over the years. Take the time when, late one evening, a fox was marked to ground, and I put in Bloody Percy, who got his name from biting so many people, though never children. After a while I heard Percy baying and waited, and waited, but he didn't come out. And as it was nearly dark the hounds had to be taken home. A factory worker called Olly stayed with me in the Land Rover.

We tried every trick to get Percy out, including the old favourite of starting the engine up and reversing so that the dog thinks it's going to be left behind. And we listened at every hole, but still no sign of Percy. Then Olly said he really had to go as he was on night duty; if necessary he'd join me to dig in the morning.

But just before he went, Olly had one more listen at a hole twenty yards away. 'Quick, shine your torch in here!' he called. 'There's a big dog fox backing towards me and it's dragging Percy, who's holding on to his nose.'

However, as we put the humane killer down on the ground ready and I shone the torch, Olly said he would not handle Percy because of his reputation. So I told him to take the fox, and that I would deal with Percy. But as the fox came up within reach Olly shouted: 'Percy, you bloody dog, let it go!' And he did. But I said, 'You fool Olly! Percy let go because that was his fox and he hates being sworn at. Now he's gone back down the hole to sulk.' Olly had handled the fox OK and shot it, but I knew that Percy wouldn't come out for some time, so it was back to the Land Rover to finish the sandwiches and coffee.

Time passed, and still no Percy. Twice I tried pushing the dead fox back down the hole, which usually works, but not that day, so it was back to the vehicle again. Then, at long last, I heard the most welcome sound of all: a dog shaking the sand and earth off its coat. I opened the Land Rover door, and there was Percy, 'smiling'.

Three days later I was again out with Olly, whose missus had put him up a special lunch. But when he went to fetch it from the back of the Land Rover I heard this terrible cursing and swearing: Percy had got his own back and eaten it all up!

On another occasion Percy was with another terrier in the Range Rover, and when Brian opened the back his son's labrador jumped in. 'Percy flew at the lab, but missed and bit my thumb, so that blood spurted in all directions. My little grand-daughter came out and immediately ran back indoors shouting: "Mummy, Mummy, Bloody Percy's bitten Grandpa. He ought to go and have an injection." But my daughter-in-law replied: "Don't worry Amelia, Grandpa's been bitten so many times, he's immune".'

The aptly named Trouble was another of Brian's terriers that once refused to surface. 'I didn't like leaving her down the hole, but I had to speak at the Hunt Supporters' Club supper that evening. So before I went I rolled up my Barbour and tucked it into the hole; and on getting home I told my son Anthony where the dog was.

'At 1am Anthony returned home with Trouble. He'd heard her growling and found her curled up cosily in my familiar old Barbour. Since then I've used that trick three times; it's the sort of thing you do instinctively if you know dogs.'

At the age of eighty-seven Brian went minkhunting for the first time, and liked it so much that he has since been out with no fewer than ten of the country's twenty-one packs. Indeed, in just a few years he became such an authority on the sport he was asked to front a video called *The Gaffer Goes Minkhunting*. Not surprisingly, Brian was the only person filmed who did not require a script.

Watching terriers work has given Brian endless enjoyment

Minkhunting became popular when the otter gained protection, redundant packs of otterhounds being used to pursue the introduced pest. At first many people were worried that hounds in pursuit of mink would disturb the otter's habitat, especially as otter numbers had declined alarmingly. But Brian was soon convinced that there was no threat to the indigenous species. 'In fact, minkhunters are a great help to the otter as mink will eat otter cubs. The otter does not seem at all bothered by the minkhounds. I've even seen one following the pack out of curiosity. And without mink being controlled, many other species of mammal and bird would suffer alongside the otter.

'What I *would* like to see done away with is all this lamping in the dark for rabbits, foxes and other animals. Night is the time for *all* wildlife to rest and sleep if it wants to, or to forage and hunt, whether it's a pest or not.'

There is no doubt that both Brian and his family have been very successful farmers and businessmen. Not only do the Forsyths now own six neighbouring farms totalling some 1,500 acres, but they also sharefarm a further 8,000 acres. Brian explained that 'with so many town-based businessmen now wanting to buy land, sharefarming is a much better option than contracting. The contractor must abide by his price, and if he cuts it too close to the bone everybody suffers. But with sharefarming, when one man provides the land, seed, stock and fertiliser, and the other the experience and machinery, as my sons do, there is maximum co-operation as the profits are shared.'

The Forsyth sporting and conservation dynasty is equally well established, Brian's family carrying on the traditions almost as keenly as he has done. 'My sons Anthony and James do as much as they can to help game and wildlife. Another thing – I bet I'm the only grandad with five grand-daughters who can all ride sidesaddle! But I don't agree with everything that goes on round here; only the other day my grandson Willie came racing around the corner here on one of those four-wheeler things, and damn near hit me in my Range Rover. But I gave him such a lecture, particularly as it wasn't the first time it's happened, either.'

Beyond the home, Brian is far from happy with the pace of change:

In the old days, very few people came out into the country. Now we are besieged by townspeople, and most of them want to run things as *they* like it, with far too much tidying up. That's where they clash with us; it's plain lack of understanding. Now there's not a barn left in Warwickshire for the swallows or barn owls, because they've all been converted into houses.

When this lady came down from Birmingham to run our village shop at Butler's Marston she didn't like the bird droppings on the pavement, so she put strips of silver paper under the eaves to stop the swallows and martins nesting there. When my old friend came to see me, he said: 'Have you seen what she's done? I don't like that. Those birds have nested there as long as I can remember.' So we both went to see this lady, but she wouldn't change. And after a while she even closed the shop down. She's been a councillor too, but I don't think she cares much for the country community.

'The otter does not seem bothered by minkhounds.'

Like almost everyone else we've also lost the village bobby, as well as Len Hall the roadman, who used to make an immaculate job of scything the verges by hand. He knew all the wildlife, and could always tell you where a fox had run through. Now, gangs of men come out with strimmers, helmets and goggles, men who care nothing for the countryside and can't wait to get home; they won't even pick up the rubbish. No wonder all the wayside flowers have gone.

The population of Butler's Marston is about 250, the same as it was in the Middle Ages, but the houses are very different. In the 1940s the council condemned a lot of thatched cottages, but now they wish they hadn't and they want to preserve anything. There's been no real balance; even nearby Stratford-upon-Avon is being destroyed. We are also having to fight to save the village Church of England school.

Everyone is in such a rush nowadays, and all most youngsters can do is watch television and copy bad things. There's no respect. Instead we have lack of tradition and lack of manners. Even many of the men on the shoot are scruffy, and that would have been unthinkable in the past. But the quality of clothes isn't there now, and people don't look after things like we did. I've still got a cap I paid 7s 6d for in 1935.

Everybody knows too much about what everybody else is doing. I don't take a daily paper. My only regular reading is *Shooting Times*, *The Field*, *Horse and Hound* and *Hounds* magazine, though sometimes I find the letters in the *Stratford Herald* quite interesting. And I don't watch television, though my wife Janet does; what do I need television for, when wildlife comes to my window? I can watch things such as muntjac deer on the ground, and hawks flying past, almost any time I want.

There is a public footpath through here: the odd serious walker with a map is usually very polite and interested in everything, but these big bunches of ramblers are often very rude. They pretend to like the outdoors, but they are the very ones destroying our countryside. They constantly demand more access, but have no idea how to enjoy or use that privilege.

Yes, I've seen the best of England. Life used to be so much simpler, with more friendship and more Christianity. The thought of Sunday shopping appals me. I can remember the day when this church was always full. I've been a churchwarden here for forty-three years, an office I inherited from my father-in-law, and apart from a break of two years, Tubbs End Farm has produced a local churchwarden for over 120 years.

Despite having fallen off his horse many times, Brian has not had any bad injuries, though sport has left him with chronic arthritis in his neck 'for which pills are useless'. But his heart and lungs are still sound, perhaps partly due to the fact that he gave up smoking in 1929, when he had an ulcer. He walks the dogs every morning after breakfast, and again in the evening.

Brian is rarely seen about the countryside without a stick, and his extensive collection contains one for almost every occasion. 'That's my cocktail party piece, a thumbstick that enables me to hold a glass at the same time. And that one will catch grandchildren as well as sheep. I got it when I bought this sheepdog from old Fred Barker in Cumberland. The dog was only £10 because it was stone deaf, though I did not know that at the time, so Fred insisted on giving me this stick. But this wasn't just kindness. I found out that the dog would only work to that stick. Sadly, deafness was her undoing because she got run over.'

But when Brian himself goes to meet his Maker there will be no drab exit from what he sees as an increasingly alien world. The man who has led such a colourful life plans to

'…the sound of the horn…is the most beautiful in the world'

go with the full fanfare of tradition. 'I don't care what any revolutionary vicar says, I want my nickname, "Gaffer", carved on my headstone, just as my wife Sybil has the family nickname "Bongo" on hers. And when I'm lowered down, I want to be "blown to ground" by a huntsman. For me the sound of the horn, especially at a funeral, is the most beautiful in the world; I've seen it bring strong men to tears. You can have either the "going away" or "gone to ground".' And there was a tear in Brian's eye when he told me: 'Last year my daughter-in-law Helen, once Master of the Warwickshire, was buried up here at only fifty years old, and the huntsman blew the "gone away". It was a great honour.'

But even without special ceremony, the congregation should be large at Brian Forsyth's funeral, for 'The Gaffer' has made so many friends in pursuit of sport and other simple country pleasures throughout England. As he has said so often, 'You only get out of life what you put into it!'

Hell-Fire and Scaltheen

In Ireland, before the days of Father Mathew, there used to be a favourite beverage termed scaltheen, made by brewing whisky and butter together. Few could concoct it properly, for if the whisky and butter were burned too much or too little, the compound had a harsh, or burnt taste, very disagreeable, and totally different from the soft, creamy flavour required. Such being the case, a good scaltheen-maker was a man of considerable repute and request. Early in the present century there lived in a northern Irish town a very respectable tradesman, noted for his abilities in making scaltheen. He had learned the art in his youth from an old man, who had learned it in his youth from another old man, who had been scaltheen-maker in ordinary to what we may here term, for propriety's sake, the Hell-fire Club in Dublin. With the art thus handed down, there came many traditional stories of the H.F.'s, which the writer has heard from the noted scaltheen-maker's lips. How, for instance, they drank burning scaltheen, standing in impious bravado before blazing fires, till, the marrow melting in their wicked bones, they fell down dead upon the floor. How there was an unaccountable, but unmistakeable smell of brimstone at their wakes; and how the very horses evinced a reluctance to draw their wretched bodies to the grave.

Other stories, equally absurd, but not quite so fit for publication, are still circulated in Ireland. It is said that in the H.F. clubs blasphemous burlesque of the most sacred events were frequently performed; and there is a very general tradition, that a person was accidentally killed by a lance during a mocking representation of the crucifixion.

Chambers', *Book of Days*, 1866

Royal Turkeys

In Berkshire is the celebrated forest of Windsor. It was formerly the property of Queen Emma; and was afterwards distinguished by William the Conqueror, who built lodges in it, and established forest-law. He himself used commonly, after the chase, to sleep at an abbey in the neighbourhood. There is now little scenery left in any part of it. Some of the finest of the old forest-trees, still remaining, stand on the left of the road leading from the great park to Cranburn-Lodge. The scenery here, chiefly from the ornament of the trees, is beautiful. The most pleasing part of Windsor-forest, is the great park; which, tho in many places artificially, and formally, planted, contains great variety of ground. The improvements of the Duke of Cumberland were magnificent, rather than in a style suitable to a forest. All formalities should have been, as much as possible, avoided; and the whole formed into noble lawns and woods, with views introduced. The great avenue to Windsor-castle, tho in a style of great formality, is however in its kind so noble a piece of scenery, that we should not wish to see it destroyed. Besides great numbers of red, and fallow-deer, this park was in the duke's time, much frequented by wild turkies; the breed of which he encouraged. It could hardly have been a more beautiful decoration. As this bird was reclaimed from the unbounded woods of America, where it is still indigenous, its habits continue wilder, than those of any domestic fowl.

William Gilpin, *Remarks on Forest Scenery*, 1794

Lunatic Destruction

At present indeed even the vestiges of most of our English forests are obliterated. Of a few of them we find the site marked in old maps; but as to their sylvan honours, scarce any of them hath the least remains to boast. Some of the woods were destroyed in licentious times: and many have been suffered, through mere negligence, to waste away – the pillage of a dishonest neighbourhood.

But the landscape, which depends chiefly on *woodland scenery*, is always open to injury. Every graceless hand can fell a tree. The value of timber is its misfortune. It is rarely suffered to stand, when it is fit for use; and in a cultivated country, woods are considered only as large corn-fields; cut, as soon as ripe: and when they are cut for the uses, to which they are properly designed, tho we may lament, we should not repine. But when they are cut, as they often are, yet immature, to make up a matrimonial purse, or to carry the profits of them to race-grounds, and gaming-houses, we cannot help wishing the profligate possessors had been placed, like lunatics, and idiots, under the care of guardians, who might have prevented such ruinous, and unwarrantable waste.

William Gilpin, *Remarks on Forest Scenery*, 1794

Feathers Out

We are glad that at a conference of ladies held in Bond-street on the subject of dress it was decided a few days ago that the plumage of small birds should no longer be considered as fashionable for robes or bonnets.

The Shooting Times, 14 October 1887

Old-Fashioned Christmas

Some idea of the ceremony observed may be formed from the following code of instructions, for the guidance of a nobleman's household in the Elizabethan era: 'On Christmas Day, service in the church ended, the gentlemen presently repair into the hall to breakfast, with brawn, mustard and malmsey. At dinner, the butler, appointed for the Christmas, is to see the tables covered and furnished; and the ordinary butlers of the house are decently to set bread, napkins, and trenchers, in good form, at every table; with spoons and knives. At the first course is served in a fair and large boar's head, upon a silver platter, with minstrelsy. Two servants are to attend at supper, and to bear two fair torches of wax, next before the musicians and trumpeters, and stand above the fire with the music, till the first course be served in through the hall. Which performed, they, with the music, are to return into the buttery. The like course is to be observed in all things, during the time of Christmas. At night, before supper, are revels and dancing, and so also after supper, during the twelve days of Christmas. The Master of the Revels is, after dinner or supper, to sing a carol, or song; and command other gentlemen then there present to sing with him and the company; and see it very decently performed.'

The boar's head and the Wassail bowl were the two most important accessories to Christmas in the olden time. The phrase 'Wassail' occurs in the oldest carol that has been handed down to us, and in the works of Spenser, Shakespeare and Ben Jonson mention is made of the Wassail bowl, which shows, that in their day it continued to form a necessary portion of the festivities. New-year's eve and Twelfth-night were the occasions on which the Wassail-bowl was chiefly in requisition. In a collection of ordinances for the regulation of the royal household, in the reign of Henry VII, on Twelfth-night the steward was enjoined, when he entered with the spiced and smoking beverage, to cry 'Wassail' three times, to which the royal chaplain – jolly priest, as he doubtless was – had to answer with a song. While the wealthier classes were enjoying themselves with copious draughts of 'lamb's wool' – as the beverage, composed of ale, nutmeg, sugar, toast, and roasted crabs, or apples, with which the bowl was filled, was styled – the poorer sort of people went from house to house with Wassail bowls adorned with ribbons, singing carols, and inviting those whom they visited to drink, in return for which, little presents of money were generally bestowed upon them.

Bell & Daldy, *Christmas With the Poets*, 1862

Drunken Coachmen

The number of old coaching men – of those, that is to say, who were accustomed to drive when coaching was the speediest and most familiar form of locomotion – is gradually becoming fewer and fewer. In 1830 Mr Stevenson was driving the Brighton Age and set a good example to coachmen generally as regards punctuality, neatness and sobriety. Before his day many were slovenly. They drove without gloves or aprons; the old night coachmen frequently wore glazed hats such as sailors wear, and had bands of hay or straw twisted round their legs; they were uncouth and careless in appearance; rough in manner and language; and much given to drink.

I recall one occasion in 1820 when the horses had been left to themselves while the coachman and guard went in to drink at an inn. The horses started off, the guard rushed out, just in time to jump on the coach, but as they were making for a pond he jumped off and broke his leg. But such instances were not uncommon, and I remember an old coachman telling me that he once met two coaches in one night without any coachman, and that he managed to stop them both without any accident.

Lord Algernon St Maur in *Driving*,
The Badminton Library, 1890

Entertaining Tops

One grows weary of the clever shop toys, things that hum louder than bees, and speak out tunes and do other feats, very soon, and the reason is easily found. The constructors have been much more intent in exhibiting their cleverness than producing a good top, and the consequence is that the more ingenious and expensive the toy, the more easily it is used. But you do not want that, for the best of your pleasure arises from the exercise of skill on your own part. So I think it quite certain that in the open air the old-fashioned tops are the most trustworthy and durable providers of entertainment.

The peg top is the top from which most amusement may be extracted. It requires considerable skill to spin it, and after you have learnt to cast well there are some good games to play with it. Everybody knows its pear-shaped appearance, and that it is cast by means of a string with a button at the end. A good top is made of very hard material, boxwood for preference, and is fitted with a steel peg, which may be long or short. At first a short peg is best, since the top is then rather easier to spin, but when you come to play at peg in the ring you will like it a little longer. The string should be of best whipcord, as hard and smooth as can be procured, and rather thicker than the whipcord sold for pike lines. A button is better than a loop at the end, as the latter on the top being vigorously cast is apt to injure the finger. Two inches or so from the other end the line should be unravelled, so that it lies nicely on the top. In winding you begin at the peg, and follow the grooves till you come near the end of your string. If the line is exactly of the right length it will then be held firmly by the button, which, on beginning, is placed between your fore and middle fingers.

Now there are two methods of casting the top – underhand and overhand. The former is easy, but useless for play, and is sometimes nicknamed the girl, or chimney-sweeper cast. In it you throw out from the hip, let the top go, and twitch back the string. But the overhand, in which you make the top describe a curve, is the truer method. To explain on paper how it is done would be very difficult; the only way of learning is to watch a boy who can do it, get the idea into your head, and learn the art by hard practice. When you can make your top sleep, that is, spin so fast and so steadily on one spot, that its motion can hardly be seen, and can take it in your hand, or on a spoon while spinning and sleeping, then it may be considered you have mastered that part of the business, and can join in a game with companions.

The whipping top is generally considered the very oldest form of top, and is a capital one for small boys to begin with. They used to be rather fond of making a whipping top for themselves. With a piece of birch wood and a pocket knife it is possible to make one that will spin in this manner; but it will not be so good as those which are turned and sold very cheaply. The whipping top is started by being twirled with the finger, and kept going with the lash. A whip of eel skin, if not the very best for the purpose, is as good as any other, and has been used by so many children that without it the equipment can hardly be called complete.

The amusement of whipping a top is rather monotonous, as there is little skill required, and few means of varying it. The only game is one wherein two or three boys all whip the same top, but it is rather rowdy. On the whole the whipping top is not half such an amusing toy as the peg top, but it undoubtedly affords much pleasure to children just big enough to make it spin.

It is so easy to spin a humming top that the subject would hardly be worth mentioning except for one point. The number of humming tops in the market is uncountable, but the old-fashioned wooden one, to my mind, the best of all, is rarely sold now. Not one of the new patent metal-topped contrivances hums so pleasantly, even though some of them are guaranteed to play a tune in spinning.

P. Anderson Graham,
Country Pastimes for Boys, 1895

Troublesome Boys

'Sir, I should be much obliged if you or any of your readers could inform me of a way of preserving my fruit from boys. I have tried watching, but never catch any. They chiefly steal my pears, peaches and green peas. Could I not put a few grains of calomel in a pear, enough to make them ill, but not seriously? They add insult to injury by shelling the peas close to my rows.'

An Injured One

Ed: Out of our line altogether, but if practicable, try an alarm gun.

The Shooting Times, 22 January 1886

PRIZE PLOUGHMAN

JOE BAINBRIDGE

HORSE-MASTER AND FARMER
Durham, Cleveland and Yorkshire

As a lad, Joseph Curry Bainbridge dreamed of owning a pair of horses; indeed he was so besotted by them he once played truant to attend a ploughing match. Unfortunately for him, someone took a photo for the local paper; this was seen by the headmaster of Harrogate Hill School, and young Bainbridge was soon spotted among the crowd and subsequently punished. But the event only served to strengthen Joe's love of the working horse, destined to dominate his life.

One of only two children and born on 29 November 1914, Joe was always close to horses because his grandfather was a blacksmith and postman, and his father was a blacksmith and smallholder. Remarkably, Joe still has his father's pre-Great War day book, the hundreds of pencilled entries from October 1910 to May 1913 revealing just how varied a blacksmith's work used to be. He worked on every day of the year, though in the period recorded only once on Christmas Day, when he provided 'frost nails'. The customers' names were always entered, and some provided regular work over the years. As usual, the shoeing of horses was a mainstay, but it is interesting to note that old shoes at about 6d each appear to have been provided more often than new shoes at around 10d each. Mr Bainbridge also seems to have been a regular supplier of glass and oil. The selection of entries on page 116 (with spellings as per book) gives the amount earned or obtained for each job or item.

The railway provided a lot of work in the Darlington area, but there was plenty of poverty, too, 'and the Sally [Salvation] Army did a lot of good. It was all walk, walk, walk then. There were trams for those who could afford it, but you never went to sleep on them, the roads was so bad. Coal was scarce, and most lighting was by gas.

(left) Joe Bainbridge senior (holding whip)

Joe Bainbridge working Dinah (left) and Bess at a ploughing match in the 1940s,
watched by judge Ilyyt Cole

	£	s	d
1 set calkers			2½
Up chains			2
Rivit hedge knife			3
1 old shoe			6
3 gills linseed oil			9
1 remove [presumably removal and re-nailing of a horse's shoe]			5
Laying cultard			8
Sharp [en] and repair harrows		5	6
1 gal of lamp oil for Corry Hill Chapel			10
1 horn burn iron		2	0
Pot damper			8
4 new shoes		3	4
1 lampglass and wick			7
Solder can			2
Frost nails			8
Iron clogs			6
Hooping gig wheel		2	6
15 hayrack rungs		2	9
Repair cow chains			10
9 cow shekels [shackles] and bolts		4	6
1½ lb clout nails			6
2 oven tins		2	10
Repair thistle cutter		5	6
Solder Jim Robson's gramaphone horn*			2

	£	s	d
Repair Mohope Chapel's tea boiler*			4
Setting plough			3
1 pair cart wheel hoops	1	5	6
1 barrel lamp oil	1	1	8
Repair poker			3
Repair fire screen and 2 grates		4	6
Repair muck drag			3
Laying cutter			8
4 new shoes for young horse		4	0
1 shovel for the district council		2	9
2 removes and repair bicycle		1	2
1 new kettle		1	6
Sharp [en] and repair harrows		7	6
Repair bicycle chain			6
2 lb wire nails			6
1 flue grate		1	3
Solder bottle			2
Repair hedge knife			8
Grinding shears			8
Hooping cart wheels		5	0
1 gate loop for Thrush Hall		1	0
Repair hay sweep		1	6
Repair sickle holder and 4 bolts		1	0
Repair hay rake bar		3	6
1 hay fork		1	4
Repair mangle			6

	£	s	d
Repair auger			4
Solder acetaline lamp			4
4 pig rings			2
1 watch glass			3
1 scythe stone			4
7 holdfasts for Limestone Brae Chapel			8
1 new pail		1	0
Iron clogs			4
Repair pig trough			3
Steeling hammer			4
1 horn burn		1	0
Hooping cart wheel		2	6
Repair bull stick			6
1 stable lamp and glass		4	6
1 fire shovel			6
Dressing young horse feet			8
Sharp [en] scissors			2
New limmers crooks**		4	6
1 door band and fitting new desk for Carsfield Council School		3	0
Lay and sharp [en] hacks for district council		1	6
Sharp [en] and set saw			6
1 new sickle		1	6
1 crib chain		1	0
Tedder teeth		1	8
1 garden spade		3	9

* Jobs undertaken on Christmas Eve.   ** Perhaps used by men who spread lime on twigs to catch small birds

'Money was very scarce and I started to help farmers, to earn a bit. But we lived fairly well for a month or two when the pig was killed. Mother made lots of black pudding and sausages with sage in. She also used to get the butcher to kill three or four sheep and cure them, just like a pig. And she soaked hare in milk for a day to take all the strong flavour out. But we never had any potatoes because Father hadn't time to dig the garden.'

Joe left school at the age of thirteen – 'you could more or less please yourself when you left' – and earned 'a shilling here, a shilling there. Then I started with the Dales pony and float, delivering milk around the streets of Darlington at three ha'pence a pint for six bob a week wages. Cream was very scarce. That was when the Zeppelins went over and they bombed Hartlepool.'

In those days wood was cheap and easily obtained, so Joe also started to earn a living through woodwork, making items such as barrows, walking sticks and garden seats 'for anyone who wanted them'. Much of his leisure time was spent playing the mouthorgan at 'bob hops' (dances). Then the family moved to Stillington, where Joe did some contract work for the iron and steel works. He describes this period of his life:

Dorman and Long employed just about everyone in the area; they even paid the doctor. I was a general transporter and used to lead a horse and cart; I bought my first for £5. The huge slag heap there kept rolling down and burning the fences, and with my Clydesdale, I repaired them on piece-work, for a pound or thirty bob a job.

At Darlington I also used to lead bricks out of the kilns. One day I found a dead tramp there. He'd gone in to keep warm and had suffocated, but he'd been drinking. Another time I went to let the cows out and discovered that a tramp had hung himself in the stackyard, apparently accidentally while climbing.

Horses were always the basis of my work, and I was a sort of contractor. It provided the money to keep Mother. I started ploughing at eighteen, and for turning an acre I earned 11s, which I could manage in one day if I always concentrated hard on the next set. I started at five or six in the morning and went on till they wanted you to, or until it was dark; you never worked on actual hours. Some people were very bad payers.

Later I earned about £5 a time to break a horse in, and if I could manage one a month I was doing very well. I became very well known for it, as I could make a horse walk into a thorn hedge just with my voice.

Joe with his Dales stallion Blake Beck Boy

Haymaking during Joe's early days

In the course of this work, however, Joe was kicked a lot, and this led to him walking badly in later years.

In 1939 Joe and his wife took on the tenancy of Sir Bedford Dorman's 172-acre Antelope Farm, Newby, in Cleveland. The place was named after the ship on which an aristocrat brought marble (which became the farm fireplace) back to England after the battle of the Nile. Joe's parents also went to live there.

As a farmer, Joe was exempt from conscription, but he joined the Home Guard, 'the LDV – look, duck and vanish'. During the war he had German and Italian prisoners-of-war working for him: the Germans were hardworking and even carved toys – cleverly made wooden, pecking chickens – for Joe's two daughters.

Also at Antelope Farm were the Land Girls Margaret Seal and Dorothy Darrell. 'They always worked hard and enjoyed a good joke. We still keep in touch. Many local Land Girls ended up marrying the farmer's son.'

At the start of his thirty-one years at Antelope Farm, Joe grew mainly wheat and oats, most of which were for home consumption. But one unwelcome crop consisted of 'umpteen bombs, some unexploded, because the farm had been made into a mock aerodrome to draw enemy bombers away from the real one at Thornaby. During a raid we all used to run under the granary steps.'

Also unwelcome were the many rats which used to live in the countryside. They were especially common at harvest time, 'but we wore leather leggings and breeches so that they couldn't run up your legs on thrashing days'.

During difficult times the horses on a farm were always among the last things to go. 'Kit Dowson's son used to say: "When poverty gets into the stable, things *are* in a poor state".'

Whereas most farms in the area had about seven or eight horses, Joe usually kept ten or twelve, all broken in by him. His horses were highly regarded and were sometimes loaned for the day or hired out for log-

Joe's Aunt Mary and friend out for a ride

ging and other jobs. They had a good feed of home-produced boiled linseed, oats, bran and hay early and late in the day. But out in the field 'they had a poor do', and had to wait patiently while Joe enjoyed his repast of home-made pork pie and can of cold tea.

After the war Joe was a regular participant in ploughing competitions, and through his great understanding of horses – 'their intelligence sometimes supersedes that of humans' – enjoyed considerable success. Joe walked his horses, pulling a plough on a rulley (a flat trailer which Joe sat on), from Newby to all the matches, for distances up to sixteen miles! This meant a very long day as each competitor usually had to plough a half-acre plot, starting at 8.30am and finishing at 3.30pm. But Joe argued that the long walk was essential 'because fresh horses were no good for ploughing as they were not settled enough.

'When you were ploughing with two horses, the most steady one walked in the furrow ahead of the ploughman, the other on the unploughed land to the left. Sometimes you ploughed with three, side by side, but I didn't like that as there was always a niggly one and they never seemed to swing together as they should have done.'

The horses, Clydesdales, were broken in at two years old and generally worked until they were about twenty years old. Joe's favourite was Dinah: 'The very day she was two I put her in the binder and cut corn. Topsy, on the other hand, was like a bull at a gate; she dropped dead in the shafts of a cart at the age of twelve when I was leading turnips.'

In those days it was nearly all spring corn, so most of Joe's ploughing was in early February. However, some fields would have lain 'bastard fallow' – this meant land which was left fallow for half the summer, between the harvesting of one crop and the sowing of the next, during which it was ploughed to kill perennial weeds by desiccation; these were prepared before Christmas. 'And we never stopped for the weather',

'Captain Ramsden always used to take his cap off to a magpie'

though one exception was the winter of 1946–7 'when all the sheep were buried in the snow'.

But no matter how dogged the character, favourable weather was always important. 'A dull day wasn't in your favour – you wouldn't plough a straight furrow in the mist.' Little wonder, then, that much superstition surrounded ploughing and farm life generally. For example, to bring good luck Joe and his contemporaries would say 'May gosling' three times on May Day, and 'March hare' three times on March 1. 'Many people meeting a magpie said: "Good morning Mr Magpie", and Captain Ramsden always used to take his cap off to one.'

One unwelcome crop was 'umpteen bombs – some unexploded'

Among his many ploughing match triumphs, Joe regards his 1946 win at the Stockton Ploughing and Hedge Cutting Society Championship as the best. But while such success was good in that it promoted his name as a horse breeder and trainer, there was little financial reward: 'The most I ever won was three quid!' The certificates were the greatest reward and the rivalry was intense. Sadly, Joe had three 'first prize tickets for cart horse colt foal' stolen at Stokesley in 1952. And in the 1970s someone even stole six of his ploughs.

Another match which Joe remembers well is the international he attended in Ireland. Unfortunately he became ill and could not plough, but while he was there he spotted the first bananas he had ever seen. 'There

Ploughing certificate awarded to Joe in 1946

were hundreds of them, so I took some back home, and the children tried to eat them with their skins on because they didn't know any different.'

Just after the war, the new tractors were generally very welcome as labour was scarce. But Joe never liked them, and when eventually he did buy one, the man he employed left 'as he couldn't stand the noise'.

Another strange sight in Newby village in those days was Joe's grey Morris, bought in 1946. 'There was only me and the builder had a car then.'

Dogs, too, were Joe's constant companions: 'I had lots of them, especially sheepdogs. They were all friends of mine, but it was bad to make a fuss of them as then they'd have no respect. One of my favourites was a spaniel, Jess. I kept her to sniff out the turkey eggs which were laid all over the place in nettles and brambles.

'I used to take old Jess with me to shoot hares and rabbits for the pot. She loved it – as soon as I went to reach for the gun on top of the kitchen dresser she went crazy. Once I lent her to a man for a shoot and he wasn't going to bother to bring her back the same day, but she barked all night and in the end he had to come over at 2am.'

On retiring at sixty-five, Joe bought the twenty-acre Bullamoor Farm, near Northallerton, Yorkshire. When that became too much he sold up and bought a bungalow in Northallerton. His wife died in 1983, and in recent years Joe himself has lived in a nursing home.

Looking back over his life – 'a very full and rich one, not financially but lots of friends' –

– Joe certainly retains an impish sense of humour. One of his favourite yarns concerns a day when he was hedge-laying: 'This man stopped and said: "I say Jack, can you tell me the way to Stokesley?" I said: "Who told you to call me Jack?" He said: "I just guessed it, old fellow." So I said: "Well guess your way to Stokesley, then!" He really thought I was the country bumpkin.

'Another time, in about 1953, old Miffy the village gardener dropped dead off his bike right by our gate at Antelope Farm.' Mrs Bainbridge covered him up with a blanket, sat by him and waited patiently for Joe and the men to come back from harvest. When they did, Joe went off in the Morris to fetch the village bobby 'who was really nervous. He asked me to put Miffy in a trailer and take him to the mortuary at Stokesley. He also said: "Will you take his boots off, too?" And I said: "I don't mind – he won't kick now!".'

Jess was kept to sniff out turkey eggs

THE FARMING PARSON

THE REVEREND WILLIAM TAVERNOR

*Staffordshire, Shropshire and
Herefordshire*

Few people still living have ministered professionally to the needs of both human and animal flocks. Yet not so long ago working country clergymen commonly farmed their own glebe, the portion of land which went with a benefice and provided revenue. One of their dying breed is William Tavernor, who simultaneously sang the praises of both church and farm for over forty years.

Originally a country parson needed a glebe to keep a horse, once essential for getting about; with the advent of the motor car, however, most glebe lands lost their importance. However, many clergymen on meagre stipends could scarcely afford to run a vehicle, and William Tavernor's solution was to make the glebe land pay for his transport. 'The car went in the coach house, and the cows and sheep in the old stable.' But William never resented the extra work because farming was in the family blood.

Born on the last day of 1916 at Grimble Brook Farm, Milwich in Staffordshire, William Noel Tavernor was the eldest of four brothers. In his first year, the family moved to the 52-acre Sprink Farm, Bradeley, near Stafford, where William spent his formative years. His earliest memory is of the threshing-machine visiting in 1919 or 1920, with a steam traction engine, threshing box and bolter at the end, and his recollection of the farm is very clear:

In those days there were always lots of spugs [sparrows] and seven-coloured linnets [goldfinches] about the fields and hedgerows. All the fields had special names, such as Plough Field, the one the government said had to be ploughed up during World War I. But the ground was extremely heavy, so as soon as possible after the war it was put back to grass for dairy cattle. Before the war it had been known as Stall Field.

William Stubbs Tavernor, William's grandfather, who established the family's flock of pedigree sheep; pictured in about 1912

Shooting Pits Field had a hollow with a steep bank at one end, where archery or musketry was once practised. On the church walls, not far away, were marks where arrows had been sharpened. Big Little Field was so named because it comprised what had been a small and a larger field. The Bullring was a large hollow, about 100 yards by 50 yards by 20 feet deep; probably originally a marl pit, it had been used for bull baiting. There was a slight mound in the centre where, it was said, there had been a stake to which the bull was tied. Another hollow in the village was called The Cock Pit, because that was where cock fighting used to take place. All the fields used to have pits or ponds in them, as had the farmyard itself, as this was essential in the days before running water.

Plough Field was 'mole'-drained with a torpedo-shaped plough pulled along a foot or two below the surface by a big steam traction engine. Only one engine was used, as there was an idler at the other end of the field, by which the engine, by a second cable, pulled the 'mole' back. Both were moved along the field as work progressed. For ordinary ploughing two steam engines were normally used.

Father had two horses, Bonnie and Bob, and they were known as 'half-legged', being a cross between a light horse and a heavy one. Bonnie was out of a steeplechaser and was the fastest horse on the road in a trap; she would allow no other horse to pass her, and when a car went by my father could hardly hold her back. Bob was her son, probably by a Shire; he was bred by an uncle.

Lambing always took place on a distant part of the farm because it was the only disease-free area, and there were no injections in those days. Father used Jeyes fluid, put on with a watering can, to stop fly strike [infestation of the flesh by maggots hatched from eggs of the blowfly laid in the fleece] and cure foot rot and strike damage. Grandfather – William Stubbs Tavernor – established our pedigree Shropshire sheep flock in 1885, when he purchased five ewes.

Among our pedigree dairy shorthorns was a pure white strain. There was no AI [artificial insemination] then, so breeding was always by your own bull, or a neighbour's. Milking was always by hand, and the milk cooled by a cold-water apparatus before proper coolers came in. At first the 18-gallon churns were taken by horse and float to the local railway station, but later they were collected by lorry. The Milk Marketing Board, established in 1933, made all the difference; before that sometimes the only use for the milk was to make butter. I can remember Mother doing that with an end-over-end churn, setting dishes and butter hands. The strained milk was fed to pigs and poultry.

William's father showed both sheep and cattle. 'He had a drawer full of prize cards. Before a show there was always lots of careful washing and cleaning, and then the cows, bulls and rams all had to be led some twelve miles; my brother, aged about eight, and the farm man walked with them. Once a bull ran away and cut Father's arm badly. But people were used to walking very long distances in those days, including to church. My uncle moved his whole farm on foot for twelve miles. There were no lorries.'

Haymaking was a time for everyone to pitch in:

We used hand rakes to turn the hay, and pikels [pitchforks] to make quiles [cocks] and pitch them onto carts and ricks. Our wooden rakes were 30in across, with teeth at 2½in intervals and a handle 5ft 6in long. The only machines were a horse-drawn mower and horse rake. There was great excitement when we obtained a swath turner.

Ricks were built in the field or the rickyard, two carts going backwards and forwards. The hay was prepared by Father and a boy, employed to save paying a man's wage, and our family and the railway men took it in in the evening, one team loading onto the cart in the field, the other unloading and pitching onto the ricks. They were given cider during the work and 10s each at the end. Old Tom was the rick builder. He always said father with a 'short' 'a', speaking to me of my 'feyther'.

Hedge-cutting, or 'brushing', was then done with long-handled hooks:

The 'brushings' were not always burnt but sometimes put to good use, placed under a stack or rick of hay to keep the bottom off the ground and prevent it from getting damp. I always did this. And corn ricks were often built on the stone mushrooms now found as ornaments in gardens. This was to keep rats out.

Brushings and the trimmings from hedge laying were also sometimes used for drainage, being laid in the bottom of a trench and covered over as a cheap substitute for pipes. This would last for a very long time. It was just one of many ways in which the small farmer always tried to save money.

Water was a particular problem in the exceptionally dry year of 1921; this was when one of the Tavernors' cows broke a leg in a furrow cut for irrigation. William describes how they treated the ground:

In Staffordshire, ponds were called pits because they formed in pits created by digging out marl [soil consisting of clay and lime] which was used to sweeten the ground. And my father caked his animals well, not only to produce more milk and flesh, but also because it fed the ground. [A cake of compressed seeds, the by-product of oil extraction, was often used as cattle feed up to the 1940s.] His chief manure was basic slag, which is sweet and produces clover. In later years I used lime at only £1 a ton after subsidy, plus slag and nitro chalk to improve the ground.

Living conditions were fairly basic at the farm, water being drawn from a garden pump, as was common in those days. William remembers the pump being pulled up to mend the valves:

The only water in the house was in a boiler beside the kitchen range. Outside we had a two-hole toilet, and we bathed in a tin tub by the kitchen fire.

We needed boiling water for the pig killer's annual visit, to help get the hairs off the skin. The pig was hung in the doorway, and there was always lots of brawn as well as hams and sides which were hung in a large larder or on hooks in the ceiling.

I went to the village school. We were not well off, but by cutting down on luxuries, such as not having water or a toilet laid on indoors, my parents were able to send me and my brothers to King Edward's School, Stafford, which was fee-paying then. I went daily and sometimes cycled the five miles. My parents were very keen on education. Mother, whose father was a farmer, won an open scholarship to Newnham College, Cambridge, to study French and maths, but had to leave when her mother became ill. She was a teacher before her marriage.

William sometimes cycled the five miles to school

But there was real poverty in some cottages. The centres of village life were the school, which was also used as a hall, the church, vicarage, head-teacher's house, pub and the village shop, where almost anything could be bought. There was no local policeman – there wasn't much need for one – and no public phone. In an emergency, one went two miles to the nearest large farm with a phone, or four miles to the doctor. During the early twenties there was no car in the village, and great excitement when one was heard in the distance. Neither were there any tractors.

My father's family were innkeepers as well as farmers; Father was also a school manager, churchwarden and lay reader. Then in 1927 he gave up farming to study to enter the full-time ministry of the church.

The sale of his 'valuable pedigree and non-pedigree herd of twenty-two cattle, two horses, fifteen registered Shropshire sheep, eight pure-bred middle white pigs, twenty-two head of poultry and twenty-nine acres of grass eating' raised just £463 11s 6d in September. Ten-year-old Bonny, catalogued as 'quiet, a good worker in all gears, well-known in the district and highly recommended', fetched £26 15s 6d. Top price for a cow was £32 10s for the red Bradeley Gertrude 3rd 'in full milk and served 27 July by Transmitter'. She had been the winner of the silver medal at Staffordshire County Show in 1927. Ten ewes, which included three winners of first prizes at Haughton Show, sold for £35 the lot, while the best ram – a yearling, and also a prize-winner – fetched eight guineas. The 'deadstock' – implements, and so on – and hay were sold in April 1928, and realised a further £152 10s 3d.

Although these prices seem very low compared with today, they were not much higher than when William's great-grandfather sold his farm stock at Aston, near Stone, way back in 1868. Then, among many lots, the best calving cow made £17 7s 6d, the best bull £10, a ram £3 15s, six lambs seven guineas, the best mare £25 10s, two rakes sixpence, a haymaker £8 5s, a hay knife 5s 6d, a winnowing machine 16s, saddle and bridle £1 15s, a four-wheeled dog cart £1 10s, best stack of hay £43 10s, best pair of pigs £2 8s, a sow in pig £4 5s, best couple of fowls 4s 3d, and 3½ couple of ducks 14s.

' . . . despite her bad feet she had somehow managed to find her way home in the night'

William found that farm sales were always sad occasions. 'They mark the end of an era and of an enterprise. But with a small farm they are more the breaking up of a family and the departure of friends. On a small farm the animals are not just numbers but individuals, often with their own personal names. Even the tools and machines are almost extensions of our own limbs and bodies. It was a very sad day for my parents and us, their children, when they sold up their stock that we knew so well. This was brought home next morning, when we woke to an empty farm. It was made worse by one old cow which had been sold to a farm some distance away; despite her bad feet she had somehow managed to find her way home in the night, and there she was, in the yard outside her shed, waiting to be let in to be milked.'

When William was thirteen his father was ordained and the family went to live at Walsall, where William attended Queen Mary's School for three years. The family then moved back to the country, to Lea Cross, near Shrewsbury, and William gained his school leaving certificate at Shrewsbury Technical College. He had 'gone through school on the science side', but then he too decided to be ordained, so he had to 'mug up' on Latin.

At the age of nineteen William went to St Chad's College, University of Durham, to take a degree biased towards theology; however, he left after one year to complete a three-year course at Lichfield Theological College.

His first job was as curate at Ledbury for three years. At twenty-six he became curate at Kidderminster, in charge of an outlying country church. He married in 1945. Then he was given an independent parish of his own, at Bettws-y-Crwyn, Shropshire, right on the Welsh border, also serving as vicar of Newcastle-on-Clun parish. In 1946, at twenty-nine years old, he was considered young for such a position. 'Perhaps they couldn't get anyone else to work in such an isolated place,' he comments modestly. On the other hand, the relatively good stipend of £400 per annum was some encouragement. But whatever the reason, the appointment certainly enabled William to re-establish his roots in farming:

'The vicarage was at 1,300ft above sea level and had 3½ acres of glebe land, which was let to a local farmer. But then, after the bad harvest of 1946 came the bitter winter of 1946–7, during which the farmer lost much of his stock. As a result he gave up the glebe, which, to my delight, he asked me to take on.' Not only did this enable William to supplement his income and satisfy his love of the land, it also increased his independence when 'cut off in the depths of the country', and helped him to 'get closer to rural parishioners. Also, and most importantly, it gave my children a farming background. Indeed, two of them, as a result, are engaged in farming today.'

In that first winter at Bettws-y-Crwyn there was so much snow William could not get the car out for thirteen weeks. He remembers it well:

The hedges were obliterated, and the floor of the house was so cold our baby couldn't crawl around. I had to carry all our supplies on my back from the village of Beguildy, two miles away in Wales, where the nearest phone was. The only person who got around easily was a young farming woman who'd been in forestry and had a caterpillar tractor. The doctor and an expectant mother both had to use her vehicle.

The postman always carried a long stick with him. He said that if he went through the snow – deeper than a man in places – he'd put his hat on top of the stick and wave it. And rumour was that a farmer had a bullock which fell through the snow, threw its head back and broke its neck.

Our water supply came to the house by a 'ram' [valve], from three-quarters of a mile below. There has to be a fair flow of water to do this, and ours came from a good spring. The water ran down an iron pipe to the ram, which closed when the pressure was strong, diverting the flow up to the house. You could hear the bump of the valve working every few seconds, but you could adjust it. In 1947 a huge iceberg, a 6ft cube, formed from the tank overflow as the water kept coming up whether it was used or not. Later I piped the overflow water away, for the cattle.

I used to shoot rabbits at Bettws, but with all the snow they got thinner and thinner. The last one I bagged smelt strongly of the yew it had been eating in desperation, and I just couldn't eat it.

Many Bettws parishioners then lived in very primitive conditions. One old boy existed in a one-room hovel with a ladder up through a trap door to his bed in the roof. And a farm with four brothers just had a ladder up the wall to their bedrooms. How they raised twelve or thirteen children in some of those houses I don't know.

During his first summer at Bettws, William made good the fences and divided the land up into several small fields:

Some of the fields were cut with a scythe

I cut most of them for hay, partly myself using a scythe and part the farmer cutting with a machine. I put some in the buildings and built a small rick.

In the autumn I bought two weanling Hereford cross heifers for £12 10s and £16. One was a Welsh Black/Hereford cross which had black eyes, so was called Panda. Another local farmer ran her with his herd, and she calved to a Hereford bull in the summer of 1949; she then gave milk for ourselves and her calf. The other heifer bought in 1947 I sold as a store [an animal kept at a steady rate of growth prior to later fattening for market] in spring 1949, for £41 at a small local auction, at the Anchor Inn.

To fit in with my work as vicar I milked at nine in the morning and nine or ten o'clock at night after everything else was finished, that is being away for the day, services and meetings. Other farmers milked at about six, so I was a bit of a joke with them and got a reputation as the latest milker in the area. But there was no problem as long as the times were regular. And there were never any crises, as the other farmers helped me out when necessary.

During the spring of 1950 William weaned his calf and bought another, as Panda was not due to calve again until January 1951. 'The new calf was brought home by a transport firm and did not arrive until late at night after a very long journey. It died, so I bought another, tied it in a hessian sack and brought it home in my car. It lived. Thereafter, whenever I bought a calf I took it home in a sack. This is now illegal, and I can't think why. Calves seemed quite happy in a sack; you tied the neck of the sack around the calf's neck and it would lie down quite comfortably, though of course it could not walk.'

After four years at Bettws, the Tavernors decided it was too isolated there. Delay in getting help in an emergency was particularly worrying, especially when William fell off his bicycle and knocked himself out. So in 1950 William took the opportunity to become vicar of Upton Bishop, near Ross-on-Wye, Herefordshire. 'You are offered a move, and it is up to you whether you take it or not. Also, after you've been in a place for so long you can feel that you are becoming a bit stale.' But in William's case the offer of five acres of glebe land was significant. Sadly, William's first wife died after only two years at Upton Bishop. Four years later William married his second wife, Vida.

William Tavernor with one of the cattle he kept on the glebe land at Upton Bishop in the 1950s

William took his stock with him to Herefordshire, where he had enough ground to rear calves, running them on until they were fat and ready to kill. He gave up milking, and when Panda calved he bought a second calf to put on her:

To stop the new calf scouring [getting diarrhoea] because of Panda's rich milk I used a trick which an old farmer told me: for several feeds I gave it half a pint of cold water before it fed from Panda, so that it actually took in less milk.

When Panda had taken to the new calf, after about a fortnight, I turned both calves out with her into the field. But Panda resisted the second calf till it learnt to suck from behind, where she could not see it. Later she let it suck with her own calf at the side, but she would only let it suck when her own did, and she would only ever lick her own calf.

Sometimes, depending upon how soon she could be got in calf again, I took the two calves off her and she reared another. Once a local farmer sold me a calf for 25s because it saved him a journey to market. Three years later I sold it for killing for £75. Being a Shorthorn/Friesian cross it took that long to fatten, unlike the two years or so taken by my normal Hereford cross calves.

I carried on in this way for the next twenty years, with Panda and later another breeding cow. After that I changed to buying two weanlings and running them on to be ready for the butcher, and I reared cattle in this way until I retired in 1988. My favourite cattle for this, for looks and performance, were black Herefords, Hereford/Friesian crosses. I picked them out and bought them in Hereford market.

After seven years at Upton Bishop, William became vicar of Aymestery, near Leominster, where he farmed more glebe land. There, the crows were troublesome in taking poultry food from the trough. One day William fired his 12-bore at them from his bedroom window: 'I bagged about six, dead on the spot, and about six more went up and came down again. I also had a little number 3 garden gun, which is less expensive on cartridges, to shoot the odd pigeon which came in to strip the brussels and cabbages.

'William fired his 12-bore at them from his bedroom window . . .'

'However, I would never let any wounded bird or animal suffer unduly. Neither would I treat any stock badly. Once I had a calf with a deformed leg, so I said let's have some veal. And I would always stun an animal prior to killing. I always had a good iron rod for the chickens. Breaking the neck of an old hen was not easy.'

Rabbits, too, had to be dealt with. To keep them out William surrounded his garden with Stockholm tar on string on sticks. 'They would never cross it.'

Tar was also useful in dealing with rats. William was told:

If you caught a rat, tarred it well and let it go, the others would soon clear off because they didn't like the smell. Another good old trick was to put broken glass down their holes so that they cut their feet. But they only went elsewhere.

Rats are much more difficult to catch than mice: if one escapes a trap it won't go near it again. But I've never had one in a church, where mice are a common problem. They invariably get in at Christmas, when the holly decorations attract them. As soon as you take the holly away they start on something else, including the candles. But if you pull the candles away from the wall you fox them.

Mice will nibble all sorts of strange things. When I was first married and had a flat in a farmhouse the mice took a fancy to whatever I put on my hair. The only way to stop it was to put the bed legs in four jam jars.

Bats can be trouble in a church, especially with their droppings, but nowadays you can't do much about those legally. In the old days you had to become extremely High Church and use incense to drive them out. That was also supposed to get rid of the death-watch beetle.

Birds occasionally get into a church. One divebombed William once, while he was giving a sermon. 'I was looking at my notes – I can never remember words – when this bird swooped over my head twice. The third time it hit me in the chest, so I grabbed it, gave it to the churchwarden and told him to let it go outside. Afterwards I said I should change my name to St Francis. I'm not sure what sort of bird it was, but it's usually a swift or a swallow that gets into a church.'

William has also had problems with bees in church, not because they stung people, but because they flew around depositing their waxy droppings all over the place.

I kept bees for many years. Once a green woodpecker attacked the hives so I put creosote on the wood to stop that. Unfortunately bees don't like me because I sweat rather heavily, which upsets them and they attack me for no reason. Once I had to wear a veil while making hay in a field near my hives. And in the early days of having bees I got stung just below the eye, with the result that one eye was closed and my face quite distorted. I had to take a funeral in this condition, squinting at the prayer book out of one eye; afterwards I was told that some relations from away had commiserated with the local people for having such a peculiar-looking parson! After that I became somewhat immune to bee stings, but always took the precaution of working with my bees well before a weekend or a special occasion!'

Humans, too, can be a pest in church. William recalls when the boys from a local public school – Lucton, near Leominster – were a nuisance at Aymestery. 'Once they played the organ and went up the tower, but I caught them and took their names. Another time they pulled out the organ stops, but the idiots had signed their names in the visitors' book, so I went up to the school and got them to pay for the re-tuning of the organ, which was unplayable because they had put the pipes back in all the wrong places.'

Once it was William himself who was cautioned for his actions: 'To renovate the church bells we should have had what is known as a "faculty" – legal permission to make alterations. But suddenly these builders offered a good discount because it was their slack period, just before Christmas. I put the proposal to the church council and they were keen, so the work was soon under way. Unfortunately an official came by and saw the bells down, so I had a letter of warning from on high. It was pointed out that if the church did not administer its own affairs well, the government would take over with town and country planning and other bureaucracy.'

A few very old-fashioned parishioners sometimes even resented the way in which William turned out. 'I was never one for a dog collar, and one day when I was not wearing it a farmer said to me: "You're not properly dressed." So I said to him: "You're not sucking a straw, but no matter." Fortunately, he took it in good heart.'

Until his last vicarage, William made all his own hay:

Quite early on, in 1951, I bought an Allen motor scythe for cutting the mowing field. This was my only machinery, apart from a truck which I made for the Allen to pull to bring in the hay. Everything else was done with handrake or pikel [pitchfork].

After cutting the grass my method was to turn two swaths into one as soon as possible, and then fairly soon to bring two of these together. The grass was then in rows about ten feet apart, and easy to turn and shake out. This made for ease of working with rake or pikel, especially if the weather was poor. I then put the hay into cocks, ready to be carted in. It was safe even if the weather broke and could stop like this for several days or more. If it had to stand considerably longer I often turned the cocks over to bring the bottom damp to the top to dry out and get the cocks onto new ground.

Mostly I put the hay under cover, and when this was not possible I built a stack or rick, which should be neither too high nor too low. The secret of rick building is to keep the centre up and then put as steep a top on it as possible. I never thatched a rick as it would be used in the first winter, and very little was wasted. I could also cut a rick with a hay knife, another art now fast going.

If the hay had to be stacked a little damp, an old trick was to put salt with it, about a pound to the hundredweight. In the forty years I made hay I never completely lost a crop, and each year I made it in at least two parts. Even so, I found that haymaking was the most nerve-racking time in farming. How my wife put up with me during it I don't know.

The rick should have as steep a top as possible

In addition to the hay and grazing, I fed quite a lot of cake to the cattle and sheep, but I think it paid. Even when there was rich grass I occasionally fed handfuls of cake to the stock, so that they would follow me, and this was very useful if they got out and went among stock belonging to other people. Some years I also grew about a ton of mangels in the garden for cattle food. And in 1976, when the stream dried up, I cut down branches of willow and alder for the cows.

For several years William also kept goats for their milk, and from 1959 he had a few sheep:

These were pure, but not pedigree Cluns. I had on average eight ewes and a ram, the latter being changed from time to time. Apart from ones kept for replacement, the lambs were raised and fattened for killing. When lambing, a most valuable thing is a cord as the lamb is so slippy slimy to pull by hand if it doesn't come easily.

Once I lost two lambs in a stream; I can only think the ewe stood in it to give birth. Another time I lost a newly born calf in a millstream, my fault for not being there when it was born, but it came sooner than I expected.

Latterly it became difficult to get anyone to come and shear, so I and my daughter had to learn to do it. She was much better at it than me; once I nearly killed a ewe by cutting through its milk vein. Luckily my knowledge of first aid meant that I was able to stop the violent bleeding.

Sheep dipping, even though neighbours were kind, was difficult. Once, having dipped outside in a thunderstorm, I had to dip again as the inspector found the rainwater had made the dip too weak. I gave up sheep in 1984 when double dipping came in, and I was getting towards seventy.

However, I was lucky to have seen the introduction of injections for sheep. Instead of having to find clean ground for lambing, as my father had done, I was able to inject all the lambs at birth and so prevent sheep dysentery, which had been such a curse.

135

Also in earlier years, I had a lot of trouble with warble fly, now largely a thing of the past. Besides putting cattle back in condition and harming the hide, it caused animals to 'gad' – gallop about with their tails in the air, when they would run blindly through fences and barbed wire. To kill the warble grub I had to rub the backs of all cattle with derris.

Another innovation which made all the difference in farming, even for me in the small way that I did it, was the rubber ring, which revolutionised both the tailing and castration of lambs. Before rings, both operations had to be done with a knife. Likewise, the use of pincers has made castration of bull calves much easier, though I once had to help a girl vet who came and wasn't strong enough. Before pincers the work was carried out by a local castrator, often a small farmer, who would rope the animal, throw it on the ground and then use a knife. He then poured a secret concoction of his own into the wound – I think it was mainly hot bacon fat. The only losers over these innovations were the people who regarded the resulting testicles as a delicacy!

Flies caused the animals to gad

In 1965 William moved to Canon Pyon, near Hereford, where he looked after five country churches and glebe land of about five acres for a further twenty-three years. It was a period of great change, when the countryside generally was invaded by townsfolk seeking, temporarily at least, to escape the pressures of modern life. With them came many problems, not least the increasing incidence of theft from churches. At Canon Pyon an alms box was stolen, but – as if by act of God – the young man who took it was fortuitously apprehended when stopped for speeding and the police saw the box on the back seat of his car.

William retired from Canon Pyon in 1988, aged seventy-one, being one of the last clergymen who worked beyond seventy. 'Today you are told to retire at seventy, though you can take a full pension at sixty-five. In my time you were given a complete freehold for life, but we bought this cottage at Kingsland just before I retired.'

Today William remains very active. He has no glebe land to tend, but still keeps a good garden, assists a daughter with her Welsh Black cattle, and is happy to help the local rector whenever called upon.

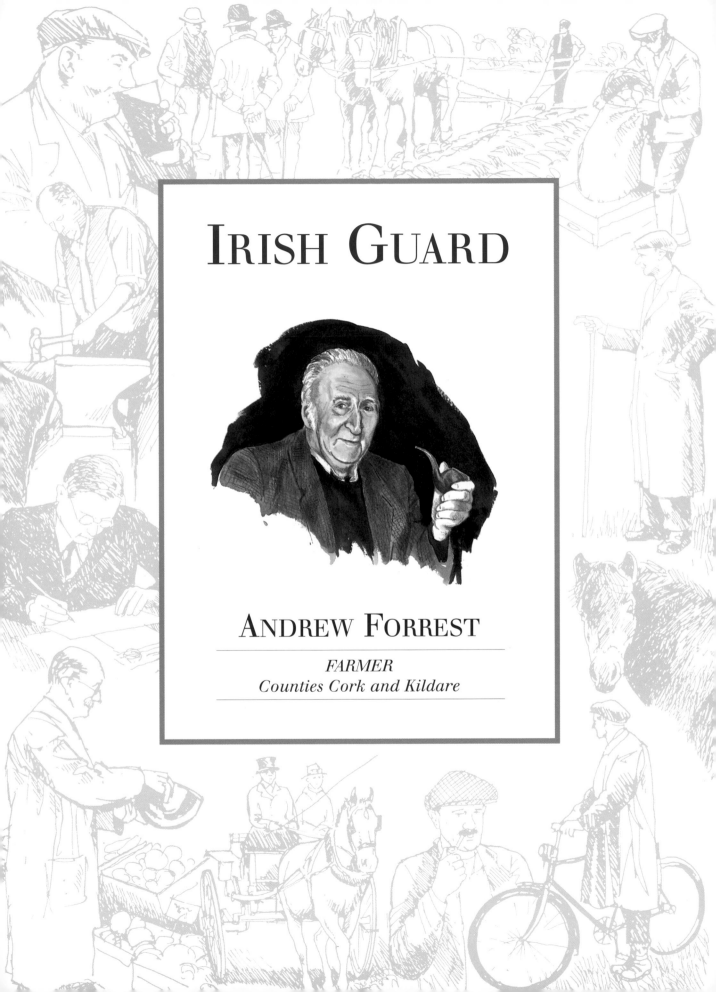

IRISH GUARD

ANDREW FORREST

FARMER
Counties Cork and Kildare

Throughout a lifetime on the land, Andrew Forrest has ridden the agricultural roller-coaster with unshakeable grip. But he has had much more than business acumen and practical skills to help him hold on: for as long as he can remember, he has had a great love of the outdoors, and has endeavoured to protect all that is best about traditional Irish country life.

One of three children, Andrew Dennis Forrest was born in north-west Cork on 6 December 1918, at Coolclough, near Kanturk, where Ireland's last wild boar is said to have been killed.

> Father had a fairly large farm – in Ireland acreages are seldom disclosed because acres on a hill are not to be compared with acres in the valley – and employed two men and a housekeeper. In those days farmers didn't work all that hard: they were employers, really. But in my view the best days in farming were already over.
>
> Mother died young, so we had housekeepers; some were far too romantic, the young ones eloping in the middle of the night, the older ones given to greyhounds and brandy. So I was sent to my grandfather's, at Coolbane twelve miles away, where I grew up. Grandad and I got on really well, and he told me lots of historical stories: I knew more about the Roman emperors than Little Red Riding Hood.
>
> We had a lovely situation at Coolbane, where the farmhouse extended into an old orchard. Grandad and I slept in a bedroom surrounded by fruit trees, and all winter the branches brushed up and down the windows. In spring Grandad opened the windows and the branches came in, soon followed by blossom. Then came the apples, and when they fell it was my job to fetch them out from under the bed. Nowadays people say that the weather used to be better, and it was! When that bedroom window was opened in the spring there was no need to close it till autumn.

With so much fruit around there were plenty of bees. 'The old chap next door had hives, and it was a great privilege to watch him work. I very soon learned that it was quick movement which got you stung.' Obviously Andrew was a good student of beekeeping because later on he became chairman of the South Kildare Beekeepers' Association, twice helping them win the world cup for honey.

At school he was less attentive. 'I started when I was about six, and was a mouse in tar until I was fourteen. Father, who was a teacher before he became a farmer, said that you were an ignorant man unless you could speak two languages, so I started to learn Irish. Later, as a young guardsman, I attended King Faud's high school in Cairo and quickly became fluent in Arabic.'

At the time the Irish countryside was full of tinkers. 'Whenever a traveller visited the school, the teacher would give a boy tuppence to take out, but we always pocketed a penny. The most welcome tinker was "Paddy the Prayers", who was well educated and knew Latin and all that. When he had returned from college to his farm he had let things go and ended up begging. We liked him because he was always sure to take half an hour off the curriculum.'

Most of the travellers were very poor and collected food and pennies from door to door. Several of the women each had their area for selling, and it was a very bad business if they went on each other's patch. 'Old Mary Ann Wallace came our way. Every morning she'd leave town with her needles, pins, thread, balls of camphor, Beecham's pills and elastic by the inch. You could order things, too – notepaper, mouse traps, bottles of ink and suchlike. She'd call at twenty houses in a day and drink tea twenty times a day.'

The travellers were also a great help to parents:

Most of them had big families, but if a woman had only an older child, she might easily 'borrow' a small one to beg, a younger child having greater appeal. Because of this it got round that they'd steal your children, so when they were about we'd never venture far from home. Our parents were also crafty about promoting ghost stories, to keep the teenagers at home.

There was much more stick discipline in those days, but that didn't stop us having a right good time, hunting and fishing and chasing rabbits. Coming home from school on Friday evening we'd decide whether to go hunting or fishing on Sunday, and we'd have to take note of recent threats of a few kicks in the backside for trespass.

For fishing we'd lime the river, a simple process, though illegal. You needed a bucket of ordinary lime, which sometimes came in big lumps, and generally we'd steal it. This was easy, because every household had it then: every farm and building was whitewashed. We always found it easiest to get things where there were no children being raised, because a certain carelessness would have set in, in that nothing was put up out of the way.

We went to the deepest pool in the river. Two boys would go upstream, and two downstream, and they would drive all the fish into this pool, which turned grey with the lime mixture poured in by a fifth boy. It was a clean-up! One bucket of lime would kill all the fish in a hundred yards of stream, including trout of every size and every other kind of fish. But they were perfectly safe to eat.

We also enjoyed the annual shoot at the great house, the gentry moving from one large estate to another. Captain Leader, near us, had maybe two hundred Guns out from all over the country. These were marvellous times for the local people because every gentleman had to have a 'man' to carry a bottle, or even two, and to refill his flask as required. At the end you were always allowed to keep what was left in the bottle. I was far too young to participate, of course, but I remember the continuous gunfire lasting three whole days. And in the evenings some of the gents would come down to the pub and stand a drink to the men, and recall events during the first war. Now, alas, the pub where the gentry and working men rubbed shoulders, where the Earl of Cavan and Jim Flur discussed the retreat from Mons year after year during the annual shoot, is closed. That once powerful little village – The Ford – just died.

Andrew can still remember the very first time that the roads were tarred:

The local man who did it was easily bribed with a few pints to drop a patch of tar into a gateway when he passed. But all the farmers were against tarring. They said it would no longer be safe to take a horse on the road and we would be back to the donkey in no time. But at least the poorer farmers were able to use the old tar barrels to house their cattle for the very first time: they opened them up and used the wood to build cowsheds. One old chap used to say 'the tar barrel is as good as the galvan eye' [galvanised iron]. Other people used them for water butts, and us children made rafts from them; so you could say that the old tar barrel changed the course of local history.

As in so many areas, the killing of the pig was 'the exciting event, albeit brutal'. As Andrew describes it:

An iron hook would be driven into the pig's jawbone and the poor animal dragged across the farmyard and slung on the kitchen table, with a man holding on to each leg – and one on the tail if you could spare him. Then the throat was cut.

There was always a 'pig sticker' for each area, and you wouldn't get a smile out of him in a hundred years. He never had enough hot water, but this gave rise to the expression 'hairy bacon' – it takes hot water to shave a man, but almost boiling water to shave a pig.

My Uncle Conor was the first man in that area to kill a pig alone. He'd been out in the Wild West for a number of years and had made some money out of inventions. When he came home the pig was to be killed, but this time he took over. One man said: 'I suppose I'll be on the gaff as usual', but Conor told all the men to stand back while he took a pan of fresh milk into the sty. He allowed the pig to drink some, then picked the pan up and took it outside so the pig followed him, over to a sheer-legs which he had prepared. There he set the pan down again, and while the pig resumed drinking, slipped a chain around its hind leg, hooked it into a pulley block and hoisted it up with its snout three feet from the ground. In that position the pig was helpless, and it was just a question of slitting its throat. All done in a simple way without that awful screeching and howling. Conor always said that brute force would get you nowhere. And you could say that that was the start of redundancy in those parts.

In every community the specialist animal 'doctor' was as important as the pig sticker: 'He had potions and ointments for almost every ailment, but much of his work, too, was brutal, including the de-horning of cattle – so they didn't hurt each other – without anaesthetic. I believe I was the very first farmer to de-horn all my cattle, back in 1947. People accused me of cruelty, most farmers laughed at the idea and some said I had gone round the bend. Now it is against the law to offer an animal with horns for sale.'

Another honoured local figure was the matchmaker, who once visited Andrew's house to make arrangements for the housekeeper:

Generally he was very successful, and used his common sense in bringing people of a like mind together. It was a very scientific job, and the matchmaker had to have a lot of inside information. And in those days, with no agony aunts, complaints were unheard of. Very few matches ended in failure.

The dowry would be given to the parents of the house where the bride was going to live. Then that same money would often be kept by for the daughter of that house to take with her when it was her turn to get married. It was not unusual for the same bank notes to change hands six or seven times, although somebody had to come up with the initial payment. And there were several marriages all depending on our housekeeper, Bridget, coming up with £600! But I wasn't surprised when she managed it, because she even steamed off postage stamps to write home to her mother.

When Bridget was saving she had a lot of trouble with her teeth, and asked the dentist what it would cost to pull the lot of them. He said that if she bought false teeth from him there would be no charge for the pulling. So she accepted, and told him to go ahead and make up the replacements. She also said there was no hurry with the upper set, but she would like the lower set quickly, please.

In due course the postman passed on the message that the lower teeth were ready, and Bridget went off in her donkey and cart [women would not be put in charge of a horse in those days] to collect them. Some time later, when a friend asked her what the teeth cost, she replied:

'Oh, not too much: I left the dentist the upper set in payment for the lower!' Obviously she was determined to get that dowry even at the expense of her appearance.

In those days the blacksmith often pulled teeth, but in an emergency the publican was preferred because he always had the best 'anaesthetic' immediately to hand.

'In those days the blacksmith often pulled teeth . . .'

At fourteen years old Andrew started working for his father:

> As well as milking, I pulled and crowned beet by hand, then forked them onto carts and lorries. It was a very tough time, with the economic war of 1932–8 between Britain and Ireland. The price of cattle went down and down, so farmers were reduced to slaughtering the stock themselves and hawking the beef around the public houses in bits and pieces. De Valera brought in the free beef scheme, but the opposition parties wouldn't eat it. Then many of us young people joined the Blue Shirts. Many friends went to live in England and Jersey – not too far away if they wanted to come home.

Guardsman Forrest in Palestine, 1938

When he was seventeen Andrew was in London to see the coronation of George VI. 'I joined a lot of World War I soldiers and others who went across. I remember standing in The Mall, where the thing that really impressed me was the magnificence of the Guards. And to think that you were here in the hub of world. There was a New Zealander behind me and he said he'd like to join the Guards. I said I would, too; and so a couple of days later we went to the recruiting office and joined up. The Irish Guards were giants upon the earth in those days, and the likes of them will never be seen again.'

It was five months before Andrew returned home, after training. He served in Egypt and Palestine before the war, his most vivid memory of the period being the wedding of King Farouk and Queen Farida:

We were stationed at Kasr-en-nil and I was among a small number of soldiers selected to represent each regiment. One day we spotted this Arab band coming over the bridge, and when they saw British troops they immediately formed a semi-circle and started to play. What a thrill it was to hear that completely Arab band strike up 'It's a long way to Tipperary'!

Well, the wedding was the greatest celebration you are ever likely to see. It went on for a whole week, and princes came from all over the place. The palace swimming pools were drained of water and filled with drink, with separate pools for whisky, brandy and champagne, and on each there were small silver boats with lads ladling out the booze. Of course, when the level fell the drink was harder to reach from the edge, and several drinkers fell in; a number of them drowned, unnoticed by the merry crowd, and weren't discovered until the 'water level' had dropped sufficiently to reveal their bodies. What a way to go!

King Farouk's wedding in 1938, which Andrew attended

When he returned to the home farm after the war, Andrew was recovering from malaria. 'For twenty years the only cure for it was to go to bed with a bottle of poteen. The tragedy is that generally the drink is no longer made as it was. In any case, there's little demand for it now, as the price of it has nearly equalled that of the proper stuff. It was always known as "a drop of the crater", because someone drinking it was supposed to be a "poor creature" [pronounced 'crater'] on hard times.'

Fortunately the disease did not cloud Andrew's judgement. On the contrary, he was founder member of the highly successful L'Avenier Chess Club, 1952 champions among thirty-two teams in the Postal Chess League (Britain and Ireland). For ten years the rooks on the board became as familiar as rooks on the farm.

In 1965 Andrew sold up and bought 'a fine place', a fair-sized farm steeped in history, near Ballitore, County Kildare. He was to have been neighbours with a long-time friend: 'A Kildare man, Tom Flannagan, and I had been through so much together – we met in the Western Desert on road watch – that we had decided we'd like to live near each other. So Tom bought a house nearby; but sadly, when he went back to England he dropped dead at a farewell party. We'd always talked about going to the pub together towards the end, but now that was not be be.'

Today, Andrew and his wife Mary still live at Moyle Abbey, Ballitore; here he found an 800-year-old skull in one of the farm fields: 'It ended up in the national museum as the earliest example of trepanning – removal of a tumour through drilling holes in the bone.'

Although Andrew is still active, his son now runs the ancient farm; however, the twentieth century races close by the window on what has become a very fast and dangerous main road to Dublin. 'On most days not a single word of the *cupla focail* [couple of words] is now heard in the nearby Crookstown Inn, whereas when I came here thirty years ago all the regulars had a good knowledge of Irish.'

Andrew outside the home where he has made many interesting additions, such as the memorial to his ancestor who won a VC in India

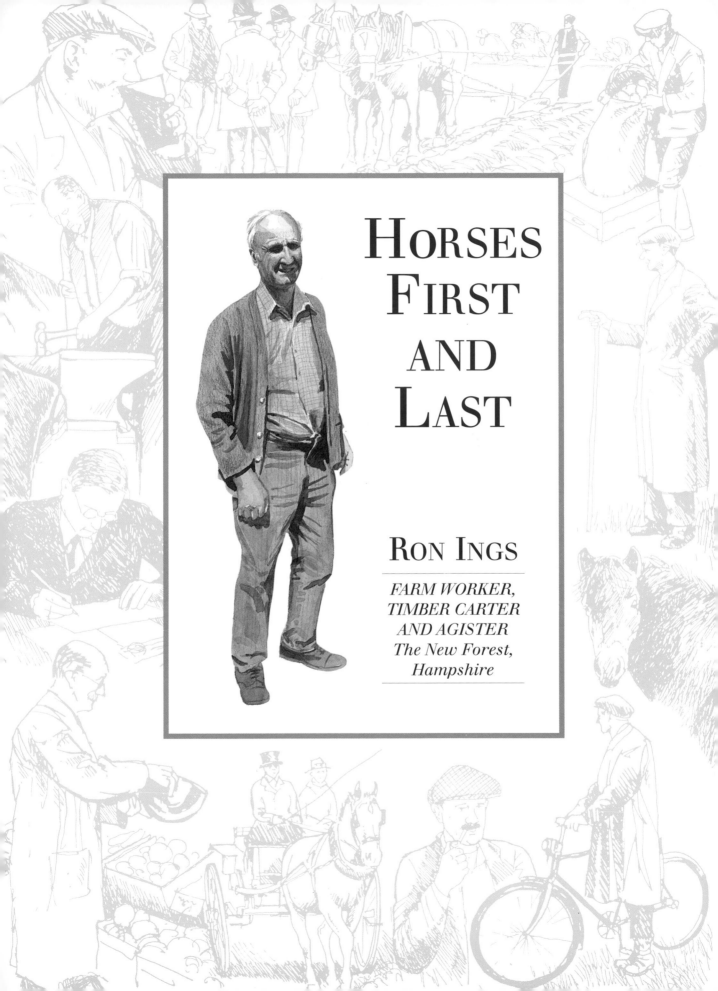

HORSES
FIRST
AND
LAST

RON INGS

FARM WORKER,
TIMBER CARTER
AND AGISTER
The New Forest,
Hampshire

It was ironic that Ron Ings' first full-time job was concerned with *mechanical* horsepower, because his lifelong preoccupation has been harnessing the strength of the four-footed beast. At the age of eight he had his own pony, 'a chestnut called Bob, which Mother bought for £2. And for the first two years I had to ride bareback – roundin' up ponies and everythin' – as we couldn't afford a saddle. But Father thought motor cars were the comin' thing, so when I left school at the age of fourteen I worked down in a garage at Fordingbridge, selling Cleveland petrol for about 1s 6d a gallon and earning half-a-crown a week.' But that lasted only a year or so, and now the lad hooked on horses is still breaking them in at the age of eighty!

Ron's lifelong close working relationship with horses is not so surprising for someone who has always lived within the New Forest, famed for its free-ranging ponies. One of two children and christened Frederick Ronald, he was born at Frogham, near Fordingbridge, on 14 December 1915. 'Father was a gardener at the vicarage, and then a butcher, delivering round the villages selling from a Model T Ford van, which I got to drive later on. I helped him with the slaughtering when I was fifteen; you just took to it as a matter of course. In those days we reckoned the weight in scores of pounds, and a pig of, say, $4^{1}/_{2}$ score would be worth about 30s. Dad would make about ten bob [50p] on that, but he would do better selling a leg of lamb for about a shilling a pound.'

While Ron attended Hyde school, about half a mile from

Ron (with his father) riding in the victory parade after World War I

home, he was always helping folk with their ponies, also some people 'up the road' who ran a few cows in the Forest. He recollects those days:

> I did some of the milking and they made a bit of butter to take into Ringwood market on a Wednesday. Mrs Chalk also made up a pat of butter specially for me.
> Mr Chalk had a Forest truck with two big wheels, but without springs, else the ruts would soon bounce a load off. His wife supplied a bottle of home-made wine and some cakes and we'd go off to cut the big ol' stumps of gorse, trim all the prickles off, tie them in bundles and take them back for the bread oven. They used to hold the heat really well.

148

Ron, a toddler at the rear, on a Royal Blue coach trip to Cheddar caves

Young Ron (front right) and family

'The horses that ate gorse grew a very heavy moustache…'

In those days nearly all the Forest horses were fed on gorse tops, the young shoots which came after the bushes were burnt. We had special chaffcutters to chop it up. The horses that ate gorse grew a very heavy moustache so that they could press down on it. It was often their main bulk feed, but they'd also get a few oats and maize.

There were several forges nearby so you never 'ad to book the blacksmith then. And if a horse was wild there was never any problem. It'd be shod on the floor if necessary, and it was still only 4s 6d a set of shoes. Nowadays there aren't the number of 'smiths, and some of those who do it are makin' a fortune with all the ridin' ponies.

While Ron was weaned on meat, his ferrets fed mostly on bread and milk:

Everybody caught rabbits then, and it was often roast as well as put in pies. Another of my favourites was the venison pasties which the forest keeper's wife used to give me. And when the cider-making gangs came round I liked to drink it as it came out the spout from the press, after straining down through coconut matting.

We were lucky to have a new house. Dad bought an acre with building permission for just £80. Then the council sunk this well 80ft deep, but it must have tapped into the main flow and drained all the wells higher up, so neighbours had to come to collect their water from us.

Our fuel was mostly wood, especially elm, but we also burnt turf. All the old cottages in the area were built with a heather turf house at the back. The turves were stood to dry in pairs.

When Ron left the garage he worked on a farm at Gorley, for 17s a week:

Three of us hand-milked forty cows – mostly Shorthorn cross – night and morning. And with a horse I drew all the mangels and marrowstem kale for the cows. If a horse or cow had a wound we used to put on Polyienta oils, and we would make up a drench for colic and other ailments. Sugar-of-lead lotion, made up from a powder, was also used to bathe wounds.

The water-meadow grass was cut with scythes for hay. They reckoned on an acre a day for a man, earning 28s for that on piece work. You started about 4am, when the dew was on the grass, as then it would cut much better. The main art was sharpening the scythe; using the stone you had to keep changing the side of the blade.

'The main art was sharpening the scythe . . .'

Ron taking out timber in the 1950s

Ron married at the age of twenty-one, and became foreman lorry driver for a big haulage firm in Southampton. This was in about 1937, in which year he used his old Kodak camera to photograph a Graf Zeppelin flying over.

Two years later Ron was declared unfit for wartime conscription because he had suffered 'a dodgy ankle' since he was a child. He describes the course his life then took:

So I went on the timber cart for the Forestry Commission, who paid us 3d a cubic foot delivered into the mill. Two of us worked eight horses, and where we used to pull the logs down the streamside at Linford we used to get bogged right down to the axles in clay.

It was all softwood we took out. We had a skid on each cartwheel and the horses pulled the logs up these with a rolling chain. And a pole ran through the cart so you could alter the length of it. We also moved wood to the charcoal burners' kilns, at 8s a cord carted in and stacked. Later on when they came to cut up some of the trees in the mill, the metal teeth of the American circular saws went flyin' all over the place because the trunks were full of shrapnel.

After the war I bought a house and a smallholding of twenty acres for £2,000, and ran a few milking cows for a couple of years. Then I started to look after a thousand Galloway cattle for Arthur Dalgety. I used to go down from my house at Linwood to drive five hundred head at a time from Rottingdean on the Sussex coast inland to Lewes railway station, from where they were brought to Brockenhurst. I branded and worm-drenched them in the station pen before they were turned out on the Forest rough grazing, generally from May to October. The first year I did that was in 1947, when it was so cold the local cattle were covered in icicles – just blowin' in the wind – and I took hay up to feed them every day.

Those Galloways were bought at Oban and really wild. If they were in pain they'd turn on you. They often used to attack the horse I was riding, upend me and give chase. One charged my wife and ran under the horse she was riding, so that the horse straddled its back. Not surprisingly, after that she refused to help me!

Once those cattle tasted grass they were away. Some wandered as far as Bournemouth and New Milton, so I had a BSA Scrambler motorbike to keep bringing them back to home base at Brockenhurst.

In 1957 Ron became one of the New Forest's four agisters, who look after all the ponies and cattle which range freely there but are all owned by somebody.

It was a hard ten years, working seven days a week all year, and on call twenty-four hours a day to attend injured or straying animals. Even when I became head agister my pay was only £10 a week, and there were no expenses except the phone and 6d a mile if you had to travel outside the Forest. You even had to supply your own car and horse.

Also, you could never please the commoners, who have the ancient right to graze their stock. In 1960 I made this pound and I wasn't very popular as I rounded up 2,400 animals and only 2,000 were paid for. One of my main jobs was collecting the marking fees. Each agister has his own area and individual tail mark – which is supposed to be done before the animals are turned out – so that you can tell where they've strayed from. My mark was one notch out the tail on the left.

Most of Ron's time as an agister was spent tail-marking and branding ponies and cattle, rounding up animals, identifying and recovering animals which had strayed or were causing damage and nuisance, and subsequently notifying owners. Today straying is much less of a problem as the animals are more contained by grids and fences.

Reading Ron's old diaries reveals how varied, and also how distressing his work could be. Sometimes people caused problems, but animals were always Ron's main concern, as demonstrated by the following selection of entries from his 1959 log:

Met senior agister at Lyndhurst to complete map of road accidents. Went to Mrs Dunlop, Sway, to notify her that one of her heifers had bad eye. Went to Avon to help commoners get their ponies out of flooded water meadows. Went to Rope Hill School to drive away cattle that were breaking into school grounds. Went to Fawley oil refinery to remove tin from pony's foot. Drove out ponies that were causing a nuisance around Lymington. Shot old pony that could not get up at Sway. Went to Balmer Lawn to look for pony reported in poor condition. Helped get dead pony out of stream. Found mare in ditch – got her out and back to owner. Destroyed mare in very poor condition. Went to Milford on Sea to catch injured pony, drove it back to Sway and notified owner. Went to New Milton to identify pony killed by train. Went to Milford on Sea to identify 11 head of cattle impounded in garden. Went to Hythe to get heifer off railway line. Motor cyclist ran into pony at Brockenhurst. Colt hunting, getting in stallions for castration. Got in cattle with bad eyes. Helped castrate bull. Got in totally blind animals with eye infection. Dragged dead steer out to roadside. Went to Balmer Lawn to get foal out of pond. Assisted police in pony-shooting case. Went to meeting at Verderers' Court to discuss erection of new road signs. Got Galloway cow out of bog. Got in blind steer. Found goat. Went to Marchwood to get nail out of pony's foot. Went to Royden Woods to destroy pony with broken leg. Went to Irons Hill to investigate blood on road. Notified Mrs Parker, Tiptoe, that her stallion was breaking fences at Ball Hill. Rounded up ponies for Beaulieu Road sales. Visited Thorny Hill Aerodrome to identify ponies that were jumping grid into private property; notified owners. Visited New Milton to try to identify ponies that had knocked man from his bicycle and killed him. Attended pony drift at Stoney Cross. Noticed unringed pigs at Burley and Minstead and got agisters Stickland and Bennet to deal with matter. Visited buckhound kennels to identify pony that had got jammed between trees. Got pony out of grid at New Park, Brockenhurst and took it to owner. Visited Longdown Gypsy Encampment and warned them that they must keep their ponies in compound. Got heifer out of garden. Found cow with her head jammed between two trees, cut down tree and freed her.

In 1960 alone he was called out to 160 road accidents involving horses and cattle, most of which were reported by the police.

The dark Galloway cattle were especially difficult to see in the dark. Now there is a 40mph speed limit in the Forest, but it doesn't stop people tearing through at night. Unfortunately for me my wife was in all day, unlike the other agisters' wives who all went out to work, and so she could receive any phone calls; so I got all their problems too, and I was in the car most of the time.

Sometimes we had two or three animals killed at once. But the worst incident I remember was when some cattle walked down onto the railway line at Hinton Admiral. The driver of the express train reported that he thought he'd touched something, so I went down to investigate. Seven cattle had been killed and I had to pick the bits up all along the line.

In the course of his work Ron got to know many individual animals:

I always knew where to find them, as they mostly kept to their own areas, and sometimes recognising them was very useful. For example, once I was called out to a road accident where this foal had been knocked down. In fact it was only stunned, but had been abandoned by its mother; so I put it in the front of the Austin 7 alongside me, but every so often it half came round, and there I was trying to keep it down with one hand and drive with the other! Anyone who saw us must have had quite a surprise. Luckily I thought I knew the mare whose foal this was, so next morning I went to look for her, and she was at her usual place. I drove her home to the foal, and when they recognised and called to each other it was wonderful!

Like all true countrymen, Ron never let his great love of animals interfere with tried and trusted Forest ways: practicality would always override sentiment. He was, for example, closely involved with the hunt – the New Forest Buckhounds. 'The cattle man I worked for was Master of Hounds, and as part of my job he would get me to hold the pack while the tufters separated the deer they wanted. In the old days the hounds were walked to all the meets, as far as Godshill, and the three Fry brothers were employed by the hunt as hound holders.'

In spite of eighty years of hard wear and tear, Ron still leaves his lodgings every day to spend several hours at his rented stables, breaking in horses and 'correcting' others. It was suggested to me that 'he likes the women who come with the horses', but there is little doubt that the animals are his first love. Indeed, his reputation is international, some of the horses he has trained having gone overseas to countries such as Germany and Denmark. Here he gives a brief account of his methods:

Ron at his New Forest stables, with his 26-year-old horse Ben (left) and a young horse being trained

155

The first thing is to get a horse to lead properly, so I start by putting it on the shaft alongside my old horse Ben. Ben is twenty-six now, and his breathin's not too special, but he's so good with young horses. I've been tipped out a few times, but never broken anythin' – only the cart. When you've got these young horses round you, it keeps your reflexes right! I'm all for a bit of action, too. When I was agister I always enjoyed goin' out on horseback and roundin' up the animals. That's why I liked watchin' the Calgary Stampede when I visited one of my three daughters in Canada!

Some people don't understand horse training, and think you're being cruel, but I hardly ever use the whip. If you get a real fighter I put the rope through an old tyre tube. But you can't lay down hard and fast rules for any animal. And it's just as important to get the animal that suits the person.

When you watch Ron out in his rough field aboard his old cart, swinging this way and that with a frisky young horse in harness, you fear for his safety now that much of his former strength has long gone. But you have only to look fleetingly into the eyes of his charge to see that the animal knows the real boss is firmly behind the reins, almost exuding power by telepathy.

'I put it [the foal] in the Austin 7 alongside me…'

156

THREE MEN, ONE ESTATE

BEATTIE, MALLINSON & STEPHENSON

FARM WORKERS AND FORESTERS
Cumbria

With the daggers of taxation and recession constantly stabbing at their hearts, Britain's great estates have needed long ownership by families with strong custodial spirit to survive the turmoil of the twentieth century. But they also owe much to the skills and loyalty of their long-serving labourers, men whose honest toil has provided sound bedrock through both war and peace. Few have contributed more than Jack Stephenson, Arnold Mallinson and Bob Beattie, whose remarkable combined service of some 150 years on Cumbria's Brackenburgh estate has helped four generations of the Harris family to remain at the forefront of estate management.

Although these three men have always lived in the same region of Cumbria and

Bob's father, William, wearing his long-service medal outside the house where Bob was born

have such an impressive record on the Calthwaite estate, midway between Penrith and Carlisle, in earlier years they also served many other employers. Robert Beattie was actually born at Brackenburgh, on 21 November 1914; his father William worked on the estate for an impressive sixty years! And despite living through times even tougher than those Bob endured, William soldiered on to the then exceptional age of eighty-six.

With nine children to feed, there were few luxuries in the Beattie cottage.

Mother made a lot of meals of sheep's head, mostly soup, and we ate a lot of rabbits given to us by the gamekeepers. We also had crow [rook] pie – using only the breasts – when the keepers shot the young birds in spring. Lots of

Bob's mother Hannah with her 'Christmas' geese

people had these pies then. And sometimes the fishermen used to come round with a cart or motorbike and sidecar, shouting 'Fresh herring', which were thirteen for a shilling.

Nearly all our clothes and clogs were handed down. Father spent all his spare time putting caulkers [metal reinforcements] on the clogs, maybe three or four a night. He got the nails from the blacksmith's shop. All farmers and workers and their families had clogs then. You'd hear the pitter-patter of the children's feet on the road as they went to school.

Being the second oldest, Bob had to supplement the meagre family income as soon as possible. At the age of only ten he began working on the home farm:

I scaled [scattered] manure in the stitches [ridges of soil thrown up by a plough] and milked by hand. For six evenings working from about four to six, or as late as ten o'clock in midsummer, I got half-a-crown [12¹/₂p]; and I worked right through the month's school holiday as well.

One evening when I was twelve or thirteen I was sent to look for sheep in a field. But there was this big stag there with the horns [antlers] on, and I didn't know what to do because it didn't even move for my dog. So I went to the keeper and he told Mr Joe [Harris], who got his rifle and shot it. The flesh was divided up among the workers, and they still have the horns hanging in the big house.

'…there was this big stag and I didn't know what to do'

On leaving school at fourteen Bob worked as a full-time labourer on the home farm. 'In those days the estate was more or less self-sufficient, with its own masons and carpenters, and there were lots of us on the land. When we went out in the morning we took bread and jam, and tea in a tin bottle with a cork in the top. This was called "ten o'clocks", even though we had it at nine. We went back home for dinner [lunch], and in the afternoon went out with our "three o'clocks" and "six o'clocks". And when milking was finished they'd bring out a big bucket of milk and we'd all help ourselves.'

At the age of sixteen Bob moved to another farm, just one mile away. But although he had been brought up on a farm and could do most things as well as any man, he was still paid only 'a boy's wage': for his first six-month contract he received just eighteen 'punds' [pounds]. So he moved around in an attempt to better himself.

One spell of eighteen months was spent in the gardens at Brackenburgh. 'There had been twelve gardeners there, but then it was down to four; the men lived in a bothy in the garden, where they saw to themselves. I left when they were cutting down on labour – the usual case of last in, first out.'

(left) Gardener Bob (centre) and (right) Bob at the cottage where he was born

During the seventeen years he was at Middle Yard Farm Bob sold his first horse, in the 1930s. 'I walked the twenty-two miles each way to Wigton sales. But it was worth it, because I bought that horse as a foal for just twenty-something pounds at Penrith auction and sold it at two years, broken in, for £35. That was the start of my bank account!'

But there was one occasion when an animal got the better of Bob: 'I was catchin' this bull. But someone put a sneck [bolt] through a latch, and the bull's head pushed it straight through my hand. I had seventeen stitches. Apart from that the only other time I was in danger was when I turned a tractor over while pulling a big stone out the ground. But I got away with it.'

Bob also drove a tractor during the latter part of the seventeen years full-time and fifteen years part-time (three days a week after the age of sixty-five) he worked in the Brackenburgh forestry department. But during that long period he never found anything interesting in the woods, 'only bloody hard work!'

Bob's wife, Eileen, came from Edinburgh in 1947 'to work with horses, but she ended up doing everything'. They met while she was a maid at Brackenburgh and now they still live locally, in one of the pleasantly situated Plumpton council houses, surrounded by open fields.

Jack Stephenson and his wife Betty live in an even more delightful place, at South Lodge, Brackenburgh, Jack's greater service of fifty-three years having earned him an estate cottage for the rest of his days. With hens pecking around the garden, the soothing hum of bees about his old hives and rural relics scattered about the outbuildings, it is hard to believe that the M6 is so close. But Jack admits that he can 'smell and hear the motorway when the wind is in the wrong direction. It cut the estate in two, and as a result some of the farms were no longer viable. The "amputated" land was either attached to other tenanted farms, or taken in hand by the Harris family.'

Jack was born at the Lessonhall estate, Wigton, on 3 March 1912. Christened John, and one of six children, he never expected to do any more than follow the furrow set by his farm-labouring father and grandfather. 'Father earned only 12s a week, but they were happier days then when we didn't have any money. You didn't need to lock your door, and neighbours would always help you out. There were many more birds then, and I always liked the spring of the year best. My favourite was the peewit, a great bird for keeping the crows away. We always used to take care to move its nest when the corn was coming through and we rolled the field with a horse.'

'My *favourite was the peewit* . . .'

Typical of the generation, the school Jack attended, Waverbridge, was very strict. He describes those times:

We often had the stick over the desk, but we had lots of nature walks. And we were more than happy playing hoops, skipping and corner-to-corner [rounders]. There were lots of trout and other fish to catch in the River Waver, with fly and worm. One time the water dried right up, and a great many fish, including big eels, were left stranded in the pools, easy to catch. I also helped Father with the snares and ferrets – I put the nets on – to catch rabbits, which we sold.

I never had much more than a bone and a couple of sandwiches to take to school. Our drink was the usual bottle of tea with a stocking on, and we all put them round the pot-bellied stove to warm up. If they got too near, the corks popped off.

Breakfast was mainly porridge, maybe a bit of bacon of a Sunday morning, and there was a joint of beef or mutton at the weekend. The Sunday tea treat was two jellies and a big tin of fruit, and there was always a bit of good farm butter.

Like most countrymen, Jack's father always kept a pig or two for fattening. 'They were just like pets, always rubbing up against you, and we used to scratch their ears. Mother kept hens, too, and we grew all our own veg. But lots of the old folk in Wigton were very poor, and some houses still had sandstone floors. Doorsteps were always coloured red with the rud fetched up from the beck. One old lady who came round selling it was known as Ruddy Mary.'

While still at school, Jack earned a little pocket money 'thinning turnips by hand for only 3d a hundred yards, but that rose to 6d by the time we came here. The farmer was always pleased to see you. I also used to help Father at Lessonhall with the milking, feeding the horses and ploughing. And the cowman had a three-wheeler pushbike which we used to go shepherdin' on, and which we had some great fun falling off.'

Jack's parents also lived at 'The Moat', Longtown. There, Jack and the other children had to attend Sunday school at Netherby, crossing the River Esk on a swing bridge to get there. When Jack left school at fourteen, he and his father went to work at Dockray Hall. He recollects the start of his working life:

' . . . thinning turnips by hand for only
3d a hundred yards'

Like everyone else then, I was hired for six months at a time. At Whitsuntide and Martinmas the lads used to congregate in Wigton for the term hirings, and when the farmers came along they'd say: 'What can'st thou do?' The two hiring fairs were the highlight of the year, and the only time you had a holiday. If you got taken on, the farmer would give you a shilling to seal the contract. For my first six months I got £10 at the end, less any subs. But you lived in at the Hall and ate with the farmer, which was considered part of your pay.

162

The money just wasn't there in them days, even for the poor old farmer. If you really worked for him he'd look after you. But if you didn't like it, at the end of that term you moved on. I stayed at Dockray for eighteen months, and during that time managed to save up 30s to buy my first bicycle, a secondhand Raleigh.

Jack then spent two years at Tarn Rigg Moor, Wigton, before moving to Anthorn, Wigton, 'at the tip of the Solway. A fellow up the village had a flat boat [punt] and a big gun which he'd take after the geese. And I used to fish in the Solway for flounders; I got them with the gripe [four-pronged fork] at low tide, and managed a living out of them. At that time I used to take a horse and cart with four bags of grain to the mill at nearby Kirkbride. While they crushed the grain into oats for porridge and cattle food I took the horse to be shod, at about 7s 6d for a set of shoes.'

After thirty months at Anthorn, Jack worked for two years for George Dixon at Easton,

The old Norton has served Jack well

Wigton. By then he was very experienced in laying hedges and drains, making and thatching stacks, and ploughing. 'Draining was all spadework then, and every wet spot had to be investigated. Tree roots, especially chestnut, were devils for blocking up along the green lane. And in the open fields we were forever replacing the tiles – in heavy ground they don't want to be too deep, and so they were always breaking because of the weight of the new machinery. It was OK while we had the horses.'

The best pay he'd ever had – '£30 a half-year' – attracted Jack to Winder Hall, Penrith, for the next thirty months. Then followed five years at Abbot Lodge, Clifton, near Penrith, where Jack married Betty, a maid in the house. There Jack earned 36s a week, and rented a nearby cottage for 4s a week; he had an AJS 500 motorbike, bought in 1935 for £10, to go back and forth.

Next came two years at Kirkby Thore, near Appleby, before the Stephensons settled into their present house at Brackenburgh, in 1941:

It was long hours, hard work and very little pay – just 34s a week – and we had two children to feed; but we were allowed a quart of milk a day and some potatoes. We were paid in cash once a fortnight. The old man, farm bailiff Faulder, used to go to Penrith to get the money and handed it out through a window if the weather was all right.

There was a big staff then. The person who used to live in this lodge got £2 a year for opening and closing the gate. And when the grandparents of Mr Joe [the current head of the Harris family] used to walk down past here, followed by the staff in crocodile fashion on the way to Plumpton church, someone even had to clean all the horse muck off the drive first. The boss then was also called Mr Joe, as each generation is called Joseph or John alternately.

Jack started as under-horseman in a team of three:

At haytime we could yoke sixteen horses and carts up. As well as generally caring for the horses and breaking them in, my duties included binding and stooking, and making stitches for potatoes and turnips. The manure in the bottom of each stitch [ridge] was put out by hand from a horse and cart. Then the spuds were dropped in by hand, and I split the stitches with a plough, covering two rows at once.

Most ploughing was done in the spring, so there were always lots of stubble fields, which were grand for the pheasants and partridges to pick over. But with the war we had to plough a lot more out. I always used to whistle and sing while I was ploughing, as the horses liked it. One I had was so obedient you could just tap his knee and he'd get down on the ground. Some of the quiet ones were sent to work in the estate woods and sawmill.

Our working clothes was always heavy cords and kittul [a sort of dark-grey denim] jackets. And in wet weather we tied brats [hessian sacks] round our waists and over our shoulders to

Jack's duties included binding and stooking

keep dry. Our clogs had laced leather uppers and wooden soles, most with caulkers bought from the local smithy. Some had a duck neb [beak] front, but rounded ones were more popular.

Mr Faulder was lame and getting on a bit, but he missed nothing and was always very particular. Everything had to come up to Mr Joe senior's standards. Faulder had a pony and trap and on Tuesday morning, which was market day at Penrith, during the years petrol was rationed, someone had to harness the pony to the trap and drive the bailiff to Plumpton station. He had to be collected again at tea-time.

One Tuesday when petrol was allowed, Faulder was driven to Penrith by his grandson. On their return he wanted to see how one of my workmates was getting on stitching a field. He took one look and blew his top, as the poor man had a dog-leg [a bad bend] in the stitches. Being a roadside field this had to be altered right away, as anyone could see these dog-legs. So I was ordered to rub the stitches down and re-stitch the field, but I wasn't very happy about this and felt sorry for my mate.

Mr Joe senior was a man who expected things to be done properly. It was nothing fresh to see him wandering in the fields with a thing that looked like a walking stick with a blade and hook on the end to dig up thistles and nettles with.

One of Jack's duties was to help clip the flock of Oxford Down sheep, 'and woe betide anyone who cut one, especially the tups [rams]. The first Sunday in September was known as Tup Sunday, when other farmers came to see the tups prior to them being taken to the ram sales at Kelso in Scotland. This was a huge effort for the shepherd, who had to take enough food for the sheep to last three days.'

Another of Jack's tasks was hedge trimming. 'All the beech hedges were dressed by hand, between haytime and harvest, and all the farm men took part. Two went with sickles to clean the bottoms of the hedges, others followed and clipped the sides with shears, and I did the tops. Then a horse and cart came and picked up the clippings. In later years I was provided with a hedge clipper run off the tractor, but it still took me three weeks to cut all the hedges, a job I took great pride in. I did this for three years after I retired from full-time work.'

Being in a reserved occupation, Jack was exempt from war service, but he joined the Home Guard. He describes the duties expected of them:

> I can still get into that uniform below the stairs, but I haven't got the boots now. We used to guard the railway, the airfield and the A6, where there was a hut, with three of us inside and three out. Any vehicle which didn't stop you gave them a ping. You had to unload when you came back into the hut, but one fellow, who was supposed to be in charge, forgot and accidentally fired a round through the roof! They were tiring days as we still had to do our own work after.

Land work was especially difficult during and after the severe winter of 1946–7:

> We couldn't start ploughing until 8 April, and even then the frost was still in some edges. It took us nine weeks, working from 7am to 9pm Sunday to Saturday. In 1962–3 there was not so much snow, but everything was at absolute starvation and the road surfaces lifted with frost.
>
> But there was always plenty of fuel on the estate as Mr Joe was a coalpit owner. Every time he had coal or coke sent down, six horses and a cart were required to collect it from the station, no matter what was going on. The greenhouses used a lot and the main house had sixty ton for the winter. When the coal, all big lumps, was neatly stacked in the open shed, the front layer was whitewashed so that nobody could pull a lump out without it being spotted.

As a ploughman, Jack always kept a close eye on the weather, and was a firm believer in country lore:

> If you saw Noah's Ark – a boat-shaped cloud formation, pointed at one end, with streaks feathering out – you knew it would be wet the following day. A big weather change would always be on the quarter-full [moon]. If there was a storm brewin', the cattle and sheep would always look for shelter and the rooks would fly round in rings and go wild. Wet weather caused a lot of extra work with all the turning of the corn stooks.
>
> Old Mr Joe was very against the introduction of the tractor, but changed his mind when he saw what it could do. I can't tell you what happened to all the horses – mainly Clydesdales – after they went to the auctions at Carlisle. Before pneumatic tyres came in, the spade-lug tractors had to have wooden bands made of beech wood put on them to go on the road, to stop them tearing the surface up.

Today Mrs Stephenson still remembers when Jack helped with the thrashing, 'when he came in smelling of rats and mice, and was so dirty you could only see the whites of his eyes. He still works five mornings a week, plucking and cleaning gamebirds (though he now has an electric machine to help), taking logs into the house, mucking out, keeping Mrs Joe's rose garden, all sorts of different jobs. He's her blue-eyed boy, and she even keeps a pair of slippers up there for him!' Furthermore, this irre-

Jack eating lunch beside his 1942 Fordson tractor at Spittals Farm, Kirkby Thore, in 1970

pressible octogenarian won a ploughing prize as recently as 1990 (for best Ins and Outs at the Carlisle and District Vintage Society match), he still shows flowers and vegetables, and hardly misses a shoot, usually standing as 'stop'.

When Jack was sixty-five, his loyal service was rewarded with the customary gold watch and pension, but the Harris family have valued his long friendship and wisdom too. When he received his long service medal at the Royal Show he talked to Princess Anne about their shared love of horses; but I think he was more proud of the fact that Mr Joe, director of the show for five years, 'laid on a coach, which was full up, to take us all there. And we've been to all the Harris children's weddings around the country, all expenses paid!' One of those children, John, is the fourth generation of the Harris family to be chief steward of the sheep section at the Royal Show. He still wears the silver RASE badge – the only one to survive – worn by his great grandfather, Joe, when he became a council member in 1905.

The third great stalwart of Brackenburgh is Arnold Mallinson, who came to work in the woods in 1938 and still lives with his wife Amy in one of the estate cottages. Christened Thomas Arnold, the son of a farmer and sole survivor of three brothers, he was born at Newbiggin Dacre, near Penrith, on 1 October 1915. Arnold's earliest memories are from Raughton Head, a few miles to the north, where he lived from the age of three or four until he was eleven or twelve.

I can still mind [remember] all them days of cutting grass for hay with the old machines, when two small farms would often join together. I helped Dad take the corn to mill to get ground into oatmeal for our own consumption and into rough maize for the farm stock. Then there were many more skylarks, and lots of corncrakes – I found their nests in our grass fields, and even a few black grouse on Lazonby Fell.

We went four miles to Dalston Station, near Carlisle, with horse and cart to get the coal.

Lighting was by paraffin lamp and water came from a garden well. We cured our own bacon and made black pudding, brawn and a good sausage. There was lots of rabbit catchin' with snares and ferrets for a bit of pocket money. We sold some in Penrith, where there were more barefoot children than out in the country.

Near our school an old chap would sit by the roadside with a heap of stones twice the size of this room. At a certain time of year the farmers took them from their fields to prevent damage to machinery and this man broke them up with ordinary hammers so that they could be used to fill in road potholes.

Each Saturday Mother went to Carlisle, where she left her trap at Dalton's Mart and then took her own butter and eggs in baskets to sell in the market. She did that for years, until Dad started to sell his milk, when we moved to Sceugh Dyke, where there was lots of fruit. He sold much of it, especially damsons. One year we had so many that half a ton went to a jam factory, and it was all hand-picked.

There were lots of tramps doing their rounds then, and sometimes droves of horses and dozens of caravans came through with gypsies on their way to Appleby Fair. They just used to let their horses into our fields, at about midnight. This lasted about a fortnight as they went through, and then they all came back again. It was a time the gamekeepers were up day and night.

On leaving school at fourteen, Arnold helped his father on the farm:

At first we had mostly British shorthorn cattle, about twenty to twenty-five, but then we gradually got into the better milking strains with, for example, Friesians. If a cow had a sore udder you just rubbed it with your own concoction, as there was no bother with the vet'nary then.

Our eighty to a hundred sheep were Suffolk cross; they were treated with Jeyes fluid or dipped if struck with the maggot. In any case, all were dipped twice a year, and each time you had to go to the local policeman to get the dipping papers to fill in. Usually he came out to see it was done properly – and that bobby went everywhere on his bike.

Then, in 1938, we came to live in a rented house just south of Calthwaite, at Firwood, and I went into the forestry at Brackenburgh. There were more than a dozen of us and I earned 33s a week. After having no proper wage with Father it was like a fortune for a while!

We sowed our own seed and had our own nursery wood on Lazonby Fell, with Norway spruce, larches and hybrids. Woods were planted out in March and April and every section had to be rabbit-fenced. Deer were a problem, too – mostly roe, but you rarely saw a stag. Another pest was pine weevils, which used to bark round the bottom of a tree and make it die. Then there were lots more red squirrels and birds of prey, especially owls. But we still see an occasional pine marten.

'If a cow had a sore udder you just rubbed it with your own concoction…'

Much later on, most of the sycamores got black blotches and died, and then Dutch elm disease took hold. And sometimes we'd fell a whole plantation if it was badly blown. The war made a big difference, as a lot of timber was felled before its proper time because felling was compulsory. It mostly went for pit props and packing cases. But our old manager fought tooth and nail to keep the old trees.

As in many other large forests, starling roosts occasionally caused considerable damage, especially through the chemical action of their droppings. Arnold recalls how the men used to stand around at dusk in an effort to keep the birds out: 'It was always in the early spring, just before they dispersed to breed. One year it was terrible, and night after night we had men out in each wood, rattling tins and firing guns. But the best thing was to put a lot of wet stuff on a good fire to get a bit of smoke going.'

Haytiming for Arnold

168

During the war Arnold often saw prisoners-of-war walking around as they worked on local farms. He remembers those times:

I was in the Home Guard and it was pretty tiring on nights, but that was only about once a fortnight as we were in groups of about half-a-dozen from the different villages.

Rabbits fetched a good price in the war, but we couldn't do much rabbitin' on the forestry. The estate had three gamekeepers and a rabbit catcher. There was always a little bit of friction

Arnold's mother and sister minding the horses while the men
were eating before they went off to cut corn

169

between the head forester and the head keeper when we wanted to work in certain areas. In the old days the keeper always came first, because estate owners had more money to spend on sport, but now there's only one keeper here and the area of forestry has increased slightly, being about a thousand acres.

In 1937 almost all the forestry on Lazonby Fell was wiped out by fire, which went right through from the Plumpton road to the Lazonby road. In those days there was no help from the fire brigade, and it was left to the workers to try to beat it out. It swept through heather with flames six feet high, and they had to fight it night and day for a week because it got into the peat and kept breaking out again. Sometimes you could hear it roaring a mile away. It was such a waste, though some of the blackened stumps were OK for railway sleepers and pit props.

Arnold married in 1942 and was given a little estate cottage.

In those days the village practically relied on the estate for work. We were a very close community, and after the war held a big village welcome-home party for the troops. I was secretary

The Clydesdale horse was the backbone of forest work

Arnold (left) receives his Royal Agricultural Society 40-year long-service medal from Princess Alice, the Duke of Gloucester's mother, in 1979; he is watched by his boss, Joe Harris

of the fund and every man away, as well as the Land Army, was given some of the money we raised through sports days, concerts and whist drives.

All estate employees were expected to beat on the shoot if required, yet those who came in specially got ten shillings each. I've done it practically every year since 1938. But we always got a hot meal for lunch. During the war there was only the odd shoot as no real rearing was allowed.

At first, Arnold worked mostly with Clydesdale horses in the woods:

All the timber used to be shifted by horse and wagon after being felled by axe and crosscut saw. The horses took it out to the road, and if they couldn't pull it, they rolled it. At the roadside we had a 'three-legs', about fifteen to twenty feet high, to hoist the logs onto the wagon. But sometimes we put a ramp up the wagon and the horses pulled the logs up from the other side. Occasionally when you went to anchor a horse up it was gone. And you couldn't go home with just one, as you need two to pull the weight. So you had to tie one horse up while you went in search of the other.

Arnold's duties were very varied and included fencing as well as sawmill work, but he always preferred being outdoors.

Mind you, getting about used to be difficult in the more remote parts, as we only had a horse or a bike for transport. Some of the old chaps used to take enough food for themselves and their horses for two or three days when the work was too distant to make it worth going home at night. There used to be a special stable up on the fell.

I was sorry to see the horses go, but towards the end, when the old horseman retired, we had to feed and muck them out ourselves, at weekends as well. Up to 1955 we had nothing but two horses, two carts and the wood wagon. Then we got the Fordson Major tractor.

Another noted machine in the area was the steam Fodden wagon, which transported stone from the Lazonby Fell quarries, some going to Calthwaite and Plumpton railway stations and then abroad. The quarries were worked by the estate, and the various colours of stone went to build local houses, the white sandstone being used for Brackenburgh mansion. The stone was loaded onto the Fodden by hand or by hand-crane. The wagon came off the road in about 1939.

When Arnold became head forester he had a team of eight men, which had fallen to four by the time he retired from full-time work at the age of sixty-five. Now there are only two men working full-time, and Arnold himself tackles only light jobs such as pruning, having been ill in recent years. The long years of sweat and toil are now only memories, but a sitting-room shelf full of accolades remains as the mark of the man. There, among special photographs, are the retirement watch and the clock presented to him when he achieved fifty years of service on the estate. But as much as anything, Arnold treasures the memory of the occasion that he received his Royal Agricultural Society long service medal from Princess Alice, in 1979. 'Mrs Joe said to me: "You've got into the royal box in one day, whereas it took me five years [the term of her husband's presidency of the show]!".'

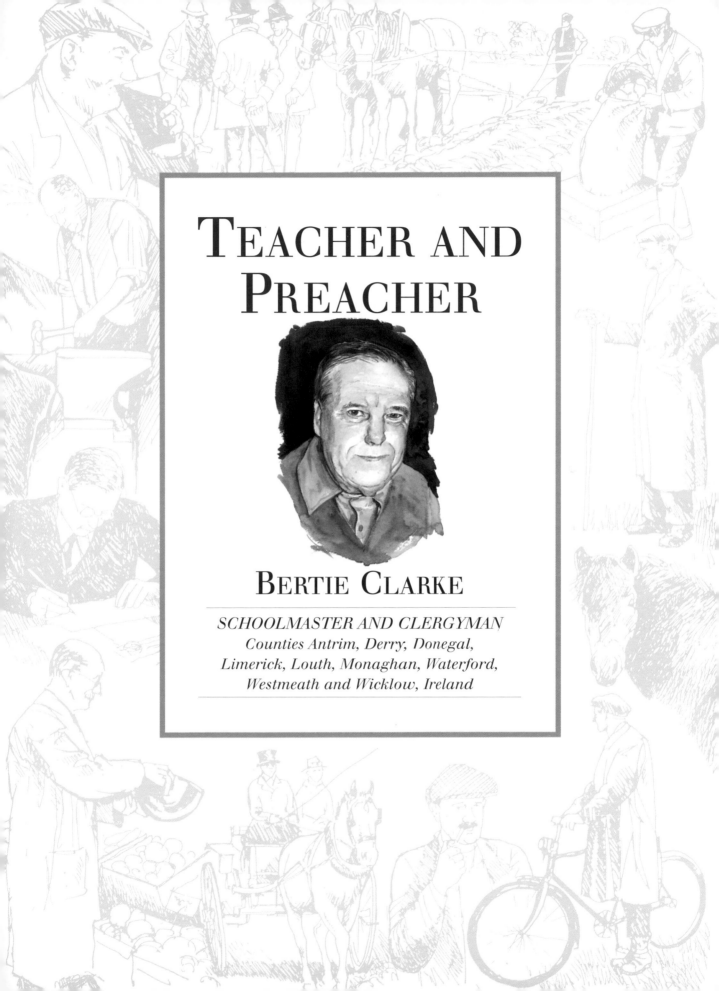

TEACHER AND PREACHER

BERTIE CLARKE

SCHOOLMASTER AND CLERGYMAN
Counties Antrim, Derry, Donegal,
Limerick, Louth, Monaghan, Waterford,
Westmeath and Wicklow, Ireland

The border between Northern Ireland and the Irish Republic certainly has great political significance, but it means far less to the countryside itself. While the two governments may manage differently through varying environmental and wildlife legislation, on both sides country folk remain equally fascinated by customs, traditions and superstitions, some of which were already old when William of Orange made his mark. But few Irishmen have come across as many of the old ways as the Reverend Bertie Clarke has. In teaching and preaching in many rural communities north and south, this citizen of two countries has become the *seanachide* (story-teller) of all Ireland.

One of seven children, Bertie (christened Robert James) was born in Belfast on 5 October 1922, 'when the Irish state was being set up'. It was an important time for his schoolteacher father because 'when they finally drew the boundary he was in Donegal and had to learn Irish'. Subsequently, Bertie too learnt and taught Irish. His earliest memories, from the age of four, are from Monaghan:

Here, shirts were hand-made by women in their cottages and taken to the local factory. Father was teaching at Rockcorry. We lived in the flat below the school and my older brother and sister had to go up and light the wood fires each morning. I remember being frightened by the big maps flapping against the wall when the window was open. Father taught in one room and his lady assistant in the other. He was fair but strict, and the class had to stand around him with their toes to a line. He used to say that the Englishman's library consisted of Shakespeare, *Pilgrim's Progress* and the Bible, but every Christmas he used to read us *A Christmas Carol*. Also at Christmas parents would send in bags of potatoes, rhubarb and cabbages to Father as a thank-you. Father also taught with Mother, at Augheygalt.

'Girls gutted the fish on the platform'

174

A lot of the children he taught at Rockcorry emigrated to America. I can still remember the parties given by the parents in the mid-1930s for those who went away. All the neighbours would come in to say goodbye.

But it was at Buncrana (which means 'at the foot of a tree-clad river'), Donegal, on the shores of Lough Swilly, that Bertie spent most of his childhood:

This was when hay-rakes were drawn by horses, one on each handle. Spinning parties were common, the women gathering in cottages to spin the carded wool into yarn. There were many shooting parties too, with a great many wildfowl and pheasants shot as there was no protection at all. But fishing was the main local industry, with Scottish and English boats. Entwhistles of Manchester used to send over boxes for the salmon. Girls – mainly from west Donegal – gutted the fish on the platform, and loaded them onto the train to Belfast and Liverpool. We lived on fish in season, and potatoes, and only had meat about once a week.

They held the hiring fairs at Letterkenny each September. A farmer from the poorer west of Donegal would bring his children and a bargain would be struck for a boy to work – for, say, six months – on the wealthier farms of east Donegal. But mostly there was only service for girls. These hiring fairs were terrible, almost like a white slave traffic with bidding for people. When a deal was made they'd clap hands, just like buying an animal. Then they'd hand over, say, a pound, as a 'luck penny'.

West Donegal people would also emigrate to Scotland for the potato season. I saw people going over there who were so poor their suitcases were tied up with string.

At Buncrana we had the regular Scottish fairs, when the Boy Scouts came over. It all became so crowded that people slept on the floors in many houses. Anything for a holiday by the sea. There was lots of dancing in the streets, but you got used to the noise and slept through it.

When Bertie went to Donegal and saw the sea for the first time he was very frightened: 'I put that down to having read Milton's *Paradise Lost*, with all those fearsome illustrations.'

Buncrana school was heated by peat fires and dried bog wood, 'better than any kindling when properly dried. Later they were replaced by the Romesse round stoves, which burnt almost anything. A few churches and halls still have them.'

Outside school the only entertainment was the country concert, so boys had to amuse themselves with the usual games, such as marbles, conkers and soccer. There was considerable innovation too, such as the time Bertie fought a sham Battle of the Boyne on the street: 'We

'…people so poor their suitcases were tied up with string.'

175

had upturned saucepans for helmets, and when I hit this boy on the head the pan went right down over his eyes. Then his mother came out and hit me. Father was cross, too, and I got a second beating from him when the boy had to be taken to the blacksmith to get the saucepan removed.'

At that time, road surfacing was done the hard way. Bertie remembers the men 'wearing goggles and sitting on sacks a-top piles of stones along the way. They were paid according to the size of the heap they'd broken. A steam roller followed them round and its crew lived in a green caravan with the name of the county council printed on the side in Irish. I remember thinking that that was what I'd like to do, as they travelled around all over the place.'

But that was not to be. After leaving school at the age of fourteen, Bertie remained at home for a few years, eventually going to the College of Preceptors in London at about eighteen years old. He remembers the 1940s clearly:

During the war years there was a lot of smuggling in our part of Donegal because we lived just fourteen miles from the border. We only had that horrible old brown bread, but Northern Ireland had plenty of the white, so grocers used to employ women and children to smuggle it in. Also we only had a half-ounce ration of tea, so that was smuggled in, too, usually in sacks along with the bread. The local women invented a thing called the Buncrana skirt, which they could stuff with contraband. The customs men couldn't touch them, so after a while they put on lady searchers.

One woman cleaned a turkey out, stuffed a bottle of whiskey inside it and dressed it up as a baby. The customs men boarded her train, but she still got through to Northern Ireland.

Another favourite trick was filling a coffin with smuggled goods. One customs officer said: 'The undertakers must be doing well – I've never seen so many coffins!'

Poteen was made in large quantities during both war and peace time:

On the farms the men sometimes couldn't work for two or three days, it was so strong. The march ditch was always the best place for a still because that was 'no man's land' and the maker couldn't be prosecuted. When there was going to be a raid the police used to come round and say: 'Keep in your dogs tonight'. Even so, the poteen men were often imprisoned.

There used to be a dreadful lot of drunks at the old wakes, with home-made whiskey handed out along with tea, tobacco and clay pipes.

After holding a number of temporary teaching posts, in 1953 Bertie was appointed principal teacher of Park Primary School, County Derry:

It was a haunted place where we heard knocking on the door. The Berrisfords had a castle there, and it was said that when a woman came to their door in the snow, to ask for help for her children, she was denied. So she cursed them, and said they would all die violent deaths. Later, all three sons jumped out of the castle windows.

One night three of us were returning from an old magic-lantern lecture and we saw the castle all lit up. Later we made enquiries, but discovered that nothing had been going on there; we were the only ones to see the lights.

[Bertie recalls an equally eerie experience in Donegal] On another occasion, two notorious robbers were using a church which was being re-roofed. One night they lit a fire inside, and an elderly couple living nearby must have thought the Devil himself was inside, with the flames flickering about the old stonework. They decided to investigate, but the old woman couldn't walk, so her husband had to carry her.

As the man approached the church his feet crunched heavily on the gravel, because of the weight of his wife. The robber inside thought it was his mate coming back with a stolen sheep and called out: 'Is she fat?'. At that, the old man dropped his wife and they both ran off as fast as they could. It must have been the first time for many years that she literally found her feet!

When Park School closed, Bertie held a temporary appointment at Ballymena Academy for one year; he then went to Drogheda Grammar School. In 1959 he was appointed to Wilson's Hospital School, Multyfarnham, County Westmeath, and taught there until 1966, when he joined Bishop Foy School, Waterford. When that establishment closed he entered the Church of Ireland Theological College, to train for the Anglican ministry.

Bertie was ordained in 1969, for the curacy of St Mary's Parish, Belfast, which involved being chaplain to Crumlin Road prison; 'this was at the start of the troubles, when there were just three of us to care for two thousand families'.

In 1970 he was appointed curate and minor canon for St Mary's Cathedral, Limerick; he then returned to Wilson's Hospital School as assistant chaplain and teacher, remaining there until retirement in 1987 when he moved to his present home in Dunlavin, County Wicklow.

Bertie is an oblate of the Anglican Benedictine Order of Elmore Abbey, Speen, Berkshire, for whom he has done voluntary pastoral work among sick pilgrims for over twenty years.

'...at the old wakes [there was] whiskey handed out along with tea, tobacco and clay pipes.'

177

For several summers he also worked as a volunteer with the late Brother Jonathan of the Community of the Glorious Ascension in connection with the North Devon Holiday Home Trust for deprived children. He has been a pilgrim visitor to the Anglican shrine of Our Lady of Walsingham in Norfolk.

Back in Ireland superstitions figured in Bertie's life from an early age, and he recounts some of them:

> Mother would never allow white flowers into the house, for fear that someone would die. And we never ate blackberries after 29 September – Michaelmas – as it was said that the Devil had then spat on them.
>
> In Donegal there was a lot of superstition attached to St Columba. And it was always unlucky if you met a white horse or a red-headed woman while you were going to market: you always had to turn back. In some parts small boys were always dressed as girls so that the fairies wouldn't take them away. And many people would never sit down thirteen to a table, including one clergyman I knew, who remembered what happened at the Last Supper.
>
> In Monaghan little girls often laid wild flowers on our doorsteps on May Day eve, to give good fortune for the coming year, by placating the fairies and warding off evil spirits. This custom continues in many parts of Ireland, along with that of Harvest Home, when the corn is gathered in. And on St Brigid's Day – 1 February – a St Brigid's Cross, usually made from rushes, is made and placed inside the entrance door of houses to bring a blessing for the year ahead.

When he was in Monaghan, Bertie witnessed the plays of the 'Wren Boys' on St Stephen's Day (Boxing Day):

> They believed that the common wren was the Devil's bird, and that the more they killed the more of the Devil's ribs were broken. They each carried a long stick with the bodies of the wrens on, and would compete with each other to see who could kill the most.
>
> These revellers travelled around the country in a van and performed in houses, where they'd sometimes be given tea. They played the violin, melodeon and penny whistle, and each was dressed according to his part. To start, Jack Straw entered in his straw costume, repeating the words:
>
> > 'Here comes I, Jack Straw.
> > Such a man you never saw
> > Through a riddle,
> > Through a reel,
> > Through an old spinning wheel.'

Next to enter was 'Devil Doubt', who repeated:

> > 'Here comes I, Devil Doubt,
> > The greatest Devil was ever out.
> > Money I want, money I crave.
> > If you don't give me money I'll sweep you all to your grave.'

He was followed by Prince George, with crown and red robe. And at the end of the performance money would be collected for charity.

'In Monaghan little girls often laid wild flowers on our doorsteps on May Day eve . . .'

Tinkers, too, often visited the houses in search of charity, though Bertie recalls that most people did not want them about. 'If you gave them a few grains of tea or sugar they'd be content, but if you gave them nothing they'd soon give you the weight of their tongue. And they were always having awful fights. I remember seeing one man in Limerick beating his wife against the pavement, both completely drunk.'

But Bertie's career also had many lighter moments; he particularly remembers his first christening. 'When this eleven-year-old waif was brought in to be baptised, I must have poured on rather too much water and he called out: "Jesus, I'm drowned!".'

179

'Then there was the wedding when the girl kept saying "I will not" because we'd got the couples mixed up and she had the wrong man. Another was too scared to speak up, but luckily the mistake was discovered before they signed the register!'

Equally memorable was the time Bertie visited an old lady who was very ill. 'I said a few prayers at her bedside, after which she suddenly declared: "I'm all right now!". She promptly got up, put on a long coat, picked up a large whip and walked out, and I never saw her again.'

But Bertie's greatest surprise of all came at a funeral in Belfast: 'It was terribly wet, and when the Reverend G. George Thomson and myself were at the grave the whole side caved in, taking us with it, down onto the coffin. We had to be pulled out!' No wonder that Bertie always preferred the country life.

The road gang lived in a caravan behind the steam roller

ALWAYS ON THE MOVE

BILL BATT

GROUNDSMAN AND TIMBER FELLER
Berkshire and Surrey

When his wife Evelyn died on his seventy-eighth birthday Bill Batt could easily have lost all interest in life. But with characteristic determination, he has kept both mind and body in good shape, to such an extent that he was able to fell his neighbour's large Cupressus tree at the age of eighty-five!

Bill's mother and sister at his Binfield birthplace

Bill's father Frank, knocking in tree wedges at Winkfield

'I *do* miss my wife,' Bill told me, 'but I told myself it was no good sitting around moping else you might as well pack it all in. The thing is to keep moving. Give in and you've had it. Do you know, there's a couple of chaps near here only in their seventies, and they pay me to dig their garden just so they can watch television all day! I can't understand it.'

One of six children, William George Batt was born at Binfield, Berkshire, on 4 February 1909. At that time his family lived in a cottage tied to the nursery where his father worked as a gardener: 'We were on the poor scale, but lucky because our house was new and there was a windmill that drew water up and sent it through filter beds into all the homes on Miss Shane's estate. Almost everyone we knew was poor, but people seemed to help one another more then.

'Sometimes I went with Father to catch rabbits for a pie. We set snares and had long drainpipes in the garden to train the ferrets. I also enjoyed playing a lot of sport and was captain of both the football and cricket teams at Binfield school.'

Bill left school at the usual age of fourteen to work for King's Bakery, Binfield. 'I greased the tins, stacked the bread when it came out the oven, and looked after the two Suffolk Punch carthorses stabled behind the bakery and used in turn for deliveries. I earned 10s a week, plus a lardy-cake for going back to feed the horses on Sunday.' Unfortunately the weekend commitment did not suit Bill because he wanted to play football for a successful local team, so after five months he left to become gardener's boy for the Reverend McNab. However, this position was not altogether satisfactory, either:

I was still on only ten bob [50p] a week. There were

two full-time gardeners and I was given all the odd jobs. Two months later Father asked: 'Has he given you that promised rise yet?' 'No,' I said, so Father put me on to Lady Haversham at South Hill Park, Easthampstead, where I got 18s a week for much the same work. It was about three miles away and I went by pushbike. And can you believe it? Each week they sent me to the bank on my bike to collect the wages of £100 or so for the five gardeners, chauffeur, maids and all the other staff.

Another of my jobs was to take the vegetables up to the house, and as it was quite a long way I used a trolley. I also had to change the flowers every week, though I couldn't see the point when the older ones were very fresh. The house is still there, but most of the land has been covered up by Bracknell New Town, and the peacocks and lovely grounds have long gone.

After two years at South Hill, Bill went to work as a labourer at Buckhurst Park, Ascot:

This work earned me a little extra money, cleaning the lake out. Then I went temporary on Ascot racecourse picking up litter, but I done so well they kept me on at the golf course, where I spent fourteen years and became head on the links.

I married at twenty-two, though there was a bit of a delay as I went down with diphtheria on the day before I was due in church and ended up in Maidenhead hospital. Then we managed to get a house behind the 6s stand at Ascot, which was where that bookie got struck by lightning and killed. The course was so waterlogged they put the races off.

During race week we had to water the course from a big reservoir, but one year there wasn't enough, so we had to put in the company's [the local water company]. But it was a hot time and we didn't want the public to know, so we ran the water at night. Unfortunately the ballcock kept knocking and woke the people in Windsor Road, who complained. Then I had to switch off at 7pm. At one time I had to turn on and off in the night

Bill aged seventeen

seven days a week for six weeks, but I got an extra 10s a week for breaking me sleep.

Gypsies used to sleep on the course in race week, to see what they could scrounge. All the locals took visitors in, and the street was busy night and day. And lots of well known people came for both the golf and the horses, including Haig the whisky man.

In 1939, to help meet the sudden wartime demand for more wood, Bill joined his father as a timber feller for Baring Industries of Bracknell. This exempted him from war service, though he was in the Home Guard. 'My wages was £2 10s a week and I needed a motorbike and sidecar – a 1927 Norton – to take Dad and me all over the place from Binfield. Later I got an old Ford.'

In those days the timber feller's work was very hard, with axe and two-man crosscut saw. But Bill had obviously worked out the best ways to tackle the work:

183

It was easier if you sharpened your tools right. The Distant was the main make of saw, and when it was sharpened nice it threw out a long piece of sawdust. You had to work well as a team with the other man, him taking a bit his side, then you, then the middle, so that you eases the tree from the top and 'e's gradually taking himself over. Me and me dad could fell and trim three good trees a day, and burn all the rubbish. When Father retired, me brother came on with me, and we were all self-taught.

When cutting downwards with a bowsaw on thinner, felled wood, such as for pit props, I always dropped an old penny in above the saw blade to stop it closing in above. This also kept the saw in good condition, which was very important as you couldn't sharpen case-hardened steel very well.

Sometimes the weather was against us. The winter of 1946–7 was so sharp and hard you couldn't get a wedge in for several weeks.

On the other hand, exceptional weather could provide the piecework timber feller with literally a windfall. This happened in 1946, when a big gale blew a great many trees down, providing Bill and his father with two months work tidying up in Windsor Great Park alone. 'Once in the park we blew a load of big beech stumps up with dynamite. We drilled holes and put about ten charges in each tree. Pieces of wood as big as this went up in the air, 'igh as a house. Fortunately I was never injured. The only time I ever hurt myself was when a wasp stung me on the forehead, made me jump and the crosscut saw ran across the back of me fingers. It's been a tough life, but healthy and good.' Bill spent many years working on Berkshire's royal estate:

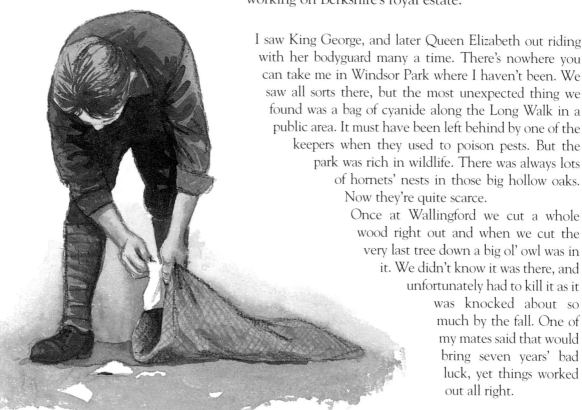

I saw King George, and later Queen Elizabeth out riding with her bodyguard many a time. There's nowhere you can take me in Windsor Park where I haven't been. We saw all sorts there, but the most unexpected thing we found was a bag of cyanide along the Long Walk in a public area. It must have been left behind by one of the keepers when they used to poison pests. But the park was rich in wildlife. There was always lots of hornets' nests in those big hollow oaks. Now they're quite scarce.

Once at Wallingford we cut a whole wood right out and when we cut the very last tree down a big ol' owl was in it. We didn't know it was there, and unfortunately had to kill it as it was knocked about so much by the fall. One of my mates said that would bring seven years' bad luck, yet things worked out all right.

On Ascot racecourse picking up litter

184

But Bill's greatest surprise came when he was working in the sawmill. 'We were cutting up this big oak when we came across a hollow inside, and in that, completely encased by some five inches of solid wood, was a toad – still alive! We'd heard stories about toads living under concrete, but how that one lived while the wood grew around it was a complete mystery to us.'

At the age of sixty Bill was slowed up by a hernia operation, after which he worked in the building industry until retiring from full-time work at sixty-five. But before long he was getting 'so much bloomin' tree and garden work', some from friends and neighbours, he decided he had to 'move away from it a bit'. So he bought the little bungalow at Elstead, Surrey, where he still lives, but remains almost as busy as ever doing jobs around the village. Well supported by his only son, Fred, he remains a man on the move.

Bill (left) with his brother (right) and colleagues at Virginia Water. They started chopping around the 960-cube oak tree at 8am and it was 3.30pm before they could even use the 7ft crosscut saw

ACKNOWLEDGEMENTS

My very special thanks go to the seventeen men who are the main subjects of this book, for being so patient with my questioning and so frank with their answers; and to their wives and families for their help and generous hospitality. I am also indebted to Phil Murphy for another evocative set of illustrations, which often required considerable research as well as artistic ability. Many publications helped me in tracking down my subjects, and I am especially grateful to the editors of *Church of England Newspaper*, *Church of Ireland Gazette*, *Church Times*, *Country Living*, *Farm and Country*, *Farmer's Weekly*, *Ireland's Eye*, *Ireland's Own*, *Irish Times*, *Scottish Field*, *Shooting Times and Country Magazine* and *The Word*. Of the many individuals who assisted in suggesting characters or in other ways I wish to thank (in alphabetical order): Hazel Aitken, The Lady Aldington, Judith Argent, Nick Boyes, Paddy Campbell, E. W. Dickinson, Marig Gray, Stephen Griffith, Joe Harris, John Harris, the Reverend Canon John Hasted, Mr Holroyd of Holroyd's Hardware, Elstead, Surrey; Mrs L. Hughes, Tom Hurney, Mrs D. Keleher, Col J. F. Kenyon, Francis Kilgeather, Judy Knight, Juliet Lance, Peter Lewis, Judith Macbeth, Peadan Macken, Rosalind Matthews, Robert McKergan, Blanch Morris, W. Mottram, Carol Muddiman, Helen Naughton, Finnbar O'Brien, Reg Pacey, Roger Pearce, Nick Phillips, Patricia Richardson, Albert Rogers, Michael Ryan, Lorcan Rynne, Neil Seaton, Peter Sexton, Mary Skerrett, Albert Smith, Ruth Swainson, Frank Taylor, Gillian Turner, Peter Varndell and Christopher Young. Finally thanks to the staff of the Sue Ryder House at Ballyroan, Ireland, to my editor Sue Hall and to my wife Carol for her help and companionship.

INDEX

Page numbers in *italics* indicate illustrations

INDEX

INDEX